Julie D. Ramsay

"Can We Skip Lunch and Keep Writing?"

Collaborating in Class and Online, Grades 3–8

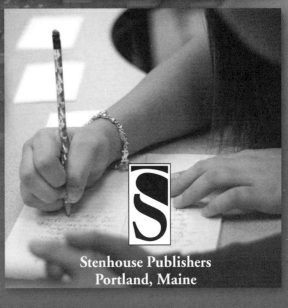

Stenhouse Publishers
Portland, Maine

Stenhouse Publishers
www.stenhouse.com

Copyright © 2011 by Julie D. Ramsay

Credits
Page 22: Figure 1.4: *Molly Moon's Incredible Book of Hypnotism* by Georgia Byng. Copyright © 2004. Used by permission of HarperCollins Publishers.
Page 23: Figure 1.5: *The Deadly Doll.* Copyright © 2000 by J. Burke. Used with permission of the publisher, Stone Arch Books.
Page 23: Figure 1.6: *Because of Winn-Dixie.* Copyright © 2000 by Kate DiCamillo. Cover illustration copyright © 2000 by Chris Sheban. Reproduced by permission of the publisher, Candlewick Press, Somerville, MA.

Library of Congress Cataloging-in-Publication Data
Ramsay, Julie D., 1970–
    Can we skip lunch and keep writing? : collaborating in class and online, grades 3–8 / Julie D. Ramsay.
        p. cm.
    ISBN 978-1-57110-847-0 (pbk. : alk. paper) — ISBN 978-1-57110-916-3 (eBook)
    1. Language arts (Elementary)—Computer-assisted instruction. 2. Creative writing—Computer-assisted instruction. 3. Critical thinking—Computer-assisted instruction. 4. Computers and literacy. 5. Educational technology. I. Title.
    LB1576.7.R354 2011
    372.6'044—dc22
                                                                                        2011007001

Cover, interior design, and typesetting by Martha Drury
Manufactured in the United States of America
PRINTED ON 30% PCW
RECYCLED PAPER

17 16 15 14 13 12 11 9 8 7 6 5 4 3 2 1

For Gene, without whose unfaltering love, support, and encouragement I would never have become the person I am today

Contents

Acknowledgments

When embarking on the monumental task of writing a book, there are so many people that you want to thank for their part in helping to shape the final outcome. No person ever accomplishes or grows without the influence and impact of others. I find it humbling to contemplate all of the people who have influenced me not only as an educator but also as the person that I've become, which brought me down the path toward authoring a book. I know that to list everyone would make these acknowledgments much longer than some of the chapters in this book. I am grateful to all of those who have encouraged and inspired me along my learning journey.

Very early in my life I knew that I wanted to become an educator. My parents, Richard and Sandra Nicks, demonstrated through their example the importance of obtaining intangible things, such as an education. They were willing to make sacrifices so that we could receive the best possible education that they could give us, for which I will always be grateful. Through their unselfish choices, I was able to become inspired at the feet of amazing educators like Cynthia Glidewell and Betty Brown, who lit the reading and writing fire within me that I hope to pass on to my own students.

Throughout my career, I have had the pleasure of working with outstanding educators. I appreciated working with Daun D'Aversa and Susan Harvill, who encouraged me to give my students as many hands-on, real-world experiences as possible. That gave me the opportunity to experience the power of breaking out of the model of a traditional classroom setting to make learning meaningful to my students. At Fultondale Elementary, I've had the pleasure of learning the importance of small-group instruction from Vicki Passantino and Tina Roberts, both of whom have patiently answered all of my questions and encouraged me when things didn't go the way I had hoped. And yes, they were right. I am thankful to Staci Moore Hawkins, who spent much of her personal time working with me, collaboratively building writing lessons for my students. She was ever willing to create special lessons for my students, depending on their needs and their interests. Staci never let the "unknown" with technology hinder her from jumping in with both feet. I am also thankful for our fifth-grade team—Amy Wicker, Jane Cox, Emily Murphree, and Dale Thompson— who helped lighten the load for me while I was writing. They attended meetings, created tests, ran copies, and wrote grade-level parent correspondences, among many, many other things, so that I could go home after school and spend time writing.

Without my personal learning network, so much of what I have written about would never have happened in my classroom. Through collaboration with outstanding educators such as Mary O'Brien, Hella Rumschlag, Laurie Loghery, Mandy Durrence, and Linda Cooper, I was always driven to learn more, try more, and live up to the high standards that shone through their students' outstanding work.

I am grateful for the plane that was delayed in Atlanta, so that I had the opportunity to meet Holly Holland, editor extraordinaire. Without Holly's unfaltering support and encouragement that I had a voice that needed to be heard in the educational community, this book would never have been written. She was always able to see the forest when I was lost among the trees. Through her probing questions and efforts to pull out the best in my writing, I have become a better writing instructor, pulling out the best in my young authors.

Of course, this book would never have been possible without my students, the amazing citizens of what they dubbed "Ramsayland." Every day I am humbled as I watch each of you grow into powerful, independent learners who will have your voices heard, now and in the future. I know that our future is safely placed in your hands as you each go out and make a positive difference in this world.

My thanks would not be complete without thanking my family for supporting me. I'm grateful to my sweet sister, Stephanie Moody, who always listens and gives the best advice, and my niece, Annalise, who keeps me laughing and gives the sweetest hugs on the planet.

What can I say about my husband, Gene? Not only did he take up all of the tasks of life so that I could write this book, but he's the best friend a person could have. He reminds me to take time to enjoy the sunsets, read great books, try new things, and explore this amazing planet. I'm blessed that we are partners in life.

Introduction

A few years ago, I was sitting in an all-day professional development workshop before the start of a new school year. My heart sank as I scanned the results of our school's standardized test scores in writing. Although our achievement results were slowly improving each year in several subjects, the low writing scores were a particular concern to me because I teach fifth grade, which is when our state first formally assesses students' writing skills.

Alabama scores students on one of three literary "modes," which are assigned randomly. The data revealed that our students not only scored poorly in the descriptive writing mode but also demonstrated abysmal grammar and mechanics skills. I had feverishly taught my students how to plan, prewrite, and write five-paragraph responses to the kind of prompts used on the state test. And according to my classroom assessments, my students had demonstrated mastery of the grammar and mechanics rules. So why were they doing so poorly on the state tests? My students didn't particularly like writing those five-paragraph responses to prompts, but they would dutifully follow the models that I provided. I thought I was teaching them writing strategies.

As my colleagues and I explored options for improving our instruction, several questions kept running through my head: How can I encourage students to think of writing as communicating with a wider audience, not just something they do to answer a teacher's prompt? What tools and resources can I use to update traditional lessons to immediately engage students? How can I weave the topics from reading, science, or social studies into writing assignments so students will comprehend the content through multidisciplinary connections? What social and emotional needs can I address in addition to students' academic needs?

It occurred to me that so often we tinker at the margins of learning instead of rethinking our basic approach. As writing teachers we vow to be tougher on grammar or to increase the number of graded genre assignments, but we seldom reexamine the purpose of writing or consider alternative formats.

Moving in a New Direction

I wanted to put writing in the center of my classroom. At the same time, I knew that I couldn't just add some assignments to my lesson planner. I needed a different way to shape writing instruction, to integrate it with the broader definition of literacy today. In addition to analyzing our school's poor performance on state writing tests, I had read reports suggesting that students across the country were falling behind many of their international peers in an increasingly competitive global economy (see, for example, Applebee and Langer [2006]). As the Partnership for 21st Century Skills (2004) reminds us, today's students need more than the three Rs to succeed. They also need the four Cs: communication, collaboration, critical thinking, and creativity.

For several years, I had used simple technology applications, such as Microsoft PowerPoint, and computer publishing to spice up my language arts lessons. Though they were just basic building blocks, these technology tools always seemed to motivate students to complete their assignments. I wondered if perhaps technology could be the catalyst that would reenergize my writing instruction as well as teach students to be inquisitive, innovative, and self-directed learners.

Experience had taught me that students learn better when they collaborate with peers and search for their own answers instead of passively receiving information from me, the "expert." I knew this, and yet like many teachers, I had often forgotten that commonsense approach when I started planning lessons. Every activity flowed through and was controlled by me. As the parable suggests, I had unwittingly neglected to teach students how to fish so they could feed themselves for a lifetime.

Truth be told, I was afraid of messing up in front of them as I used new technologies, which is why I usually returned to my traditional methods and lessons. But with technology I often had to play the fool. There was no other way to learn new software and applications than to fumble around with them, sometimes succeeding but often failing and having to try again. To my amusement and amazement, I discovered that students learned more from these experiences than from any of my "perfect" lessons. I remember the time during an out-of-state education conference when one of the students who accompanied me on the trip spotted a newspaper with the headline "Allow Students to Fail." Matthew was outraged by the suggestion that schools might give up on students until another fifth grader, Rachel, shared her perspective on the statement. Rachel said that she had often observed my mistakes in applying technology in our classroom. She talked about all of the cool, new things she had tried as a result because she knew it was okay "to not get things right" at the beginning.

Such comments encouraged me to continue exploring this new frontier of learning with my students. I started to shift my mind-set of thinking of technology as an extra and instead used it to reimagine how and what we could learn and communicate. For example, when I acquired an interactive whiteboard, I realized that it would just be a glorified chalkboard if I used it solely to disseminate information. Its power comes from the different ways it enables learners to connect with and respond to ideas. So instead of being the only one using the interactive whiteboard, I put it into the hands of the students, letting them create and interact directly with different ideas. When you examine how students spend their free time simultaneously e-mailing, texting, blogging, searching, networking, and gaming, you'll realize that all of those activities are "illuminated" by technology. Students are constantly interacting with one another and the content that interests them. They learn content that is relevant and meaningful to them (Metiri Group 2008).

So I decided to help my students build on those shared practices. Starting with simple word-processing and publishing tools, we expanded to digital storytelling, distance learning, interactive editing, and a range of activities that incorporated multiple formats for learning and communicating information. My students became my partners as we developed rubrics for evaluating their use of technology as well as their fluency in writing. We formed a new community of writers who became adept at crafting, editing, revising, and sharing good writing in a wide range of genres and media.

My students' standardized test scores in writing improved not only in each of the modes but also in the area of grammar and mechanics. More important, they became excited about learning, creating, and collaborating. No longer did students complain about writing assignments. Instead, with the tools of technology at our disposal, they started asking for more!

One of my students, Brooke, describes eloquently the benefits of writing with technology: "Writing is more than just preparing for tests like ARMT [Alabama Reading and Math Test]; it is preparation for life. We feel that we have more of an opportunity to voice our ideas to others. All of our ideas are student produced because Mrs. Ramsay lets us lead her in projects.

"I actually feel that I am able to communicate with others better the more that I write. I feel that all classes should write with technology because it's a skill necessary for life."

Where to Start?

When considering all the software and online tools that are available to teachers, we can quickly get overwhelmed by the choices. It's like trying to take a sip of water from an open fire hydrant. It's easy to feel oversaturated. But if we step back from the flow, we realize that we don't have to try everything at once. We just need to be willing to adapt. Flashy electronic tools are no substitute for strong relationships and richly layered instruction. They are merely the means to an end: engaging students.

As teachers today, our greatest challenge is not getting up to speed with technology, it's learning how to give up control. I'll never forget the conversation that showed me the wisdom of this more inclusive approach to teaching. Late one morning, while my class attended music, a small group of my fifth graders was working on a digital storytelling project. This small group got permission from the music teacher to return to our classroom so that they could record their digital stories in relative silence. When the period ended, I was debating how to bring both groups back together without leaving some students unsupervised. That's when Elizabeth, one of my students who had already finished her part of the recording, offered to help.

"Mrs. Ramsay," she said, "I'll go get them and watch them in the hall while you let the other students finish recording in a quiet classroom."

For a split second, I thought, "Wow, great solution."

Then Elizabeth said, "Wait. I'm a student." We both started laughing. It was so exciting to see how my formerly dependent students were quickly becoming confident and resourceful learners and leaders.

Over time I realized that the more I involved students in shaping their own education, the greater all of our expectations grew. One afternoon, for example, after I had finished conferencing with a small group of four students about their writing, I looked around the classroom to see whom I needed to work with next. I noticed that another four-student group was using an online search engine to locate background information.

"I never knew that Betsy Ross was a widow twice before she was thirty years old and that she ran her own business," Molly told her peers. "I don't know if I could have done that, especially in that difficult time period. It would have been so easy to have just given up."

Another group of four students was busy scanning the artwork to include in their digital story.

"Be sure to turn the picture the right way so people can read the words," Kevin reminded his peers. "That's kinda the point to these comic drawings."

Four students were using the laptop computer and a microphone to record the voice portion of their project. All of a sudden they said, "Quiet on the set!" and the room hushed immediately out of respect for the production.

Another two students were creating a video game to support their writing. Steven told Brooke, "I can work on this at home tonight. I'll work on this level and you can see it tomorrow."

"Sure," Brooke replied. "I'll be here early so we can look at it together and make any changes and then I'll work on the next level tomorrow night. Is that okay with you?"

I immediately had a flashback and realized how much my classroom had changed. Instead of being teacher centered, with all assignments and ideas flowing from my central command, the instruction and assessment now revolved around my students and their developing independence. Through a substantive switch of my teaching focus and thoughtful implementation of technology, my students have gained the power to think deeply and uniquely, to synthesize information and apply knowledge, and to collaborate while learning how to direct their education. In the past few years my students have presented at multiple international education conferences where they have confidently explained the importance of their work to educators, students, and parents in the global community. The presentations and the audio and visual interviews that resulted from these appearances provide professional development and models of technology-enhanced learning for many other school districts.

What You'll Find in This Book

In the following chapters, I share some of the lessons from our work together. Starting with our first experimental steps and expanding as we added new tools and content over several years, we built a foundation that continues to evolve with each class of students. I've designed the book to show you how to weave technology into common writing standards for the intermediate grades.

Throughout this book you will see the conversations, projects, tools, and obstacles that accompanied us on this learning journey. Although this journey primarily occurred during one specific school year, I've also included snapshots of the ways that a project or concept has evolved and expanded within my classroom in subsequent years to show that this is an ongoing learning process. I have also included reflections from students or fellow teachers to give you a different point of view on the topics I discuss.

Keep in mind that the practices, procedures, and tools that I refer to in this book were current at the time of the writing. I apologize if any of the Web sites or other information included have changed by the time of publication.

At the beginning of each chapter, I have summarized the standards, skills, and technology applications addressed within that chapter. I did this to make it easier to find quick connections to your curriculum. As I stress throughout the book, the tools aren't the most important part of this book—good teaching that reaches today's students is the main focus.

Whether you have an open-ended curriculum or very prescriptive subject requirements, as we do in the district where I teach, you will find tools and projects than can raise the roof on learning in your classroom and have your students begging to skip lunch and keep writing.

CHAPTER

1

Writing Reimagined

As I began actively integrating technology into our classroom writing curriculum, I knew that I had to do the following:

- Build students' knowledge of narrative, descriptive, and expository modes of writing to prepare them for the state's annual writing exam in February
- Weave genres such as poetry, letters, and public service announcements through the required modes of writing while also following the school district's prescriptive pacing guide for writing instruction
- Develop students' understanding and use of proper writing mechanics (capitalization,

Note to readers: The skills and tools listed below are ones I have used with my students. In many cases, you can substitute another technology application or a different lesson to use with your students. Even in my own classroom, I make adaptations from year to year depending on the students and their needs.

Standards and Skills
- Letter writing
- Grammar usage and mechanics
- Writing purpose and audience
- Communication and collaboration
- Digital citizenship
- Descriptive writing
- Self-assessment
- Technology operations and concepts

Technology Tools
- Microsoft Word
- Wallwisher (www.wallwisher.com)
- Digital camera
- Interactive whiteboard
- Document camera
- Scanner
- Moodle (http://moodle.org)
- Class Web site

usage, and punctuation, all of which were weaknesses noticed in our standardized test scores)

- Guide students' understanding of language expression (sentence structure, prewriting, content and organization, and thinking skills)

I also overlaid my goals for the affective dimensions of learning. I knew that I wanted students to do the following:

- Learn to collaborate with peers and people outside the school community while assuming different roles as leaders and problem solvers
- Develop good organization, time management, and planning skills
- Cultivate curiosity and deep thinking
- Question the purpose of what they were learning
- Prepare for the world outside the classroom

Finally, I layered the state technology content standards, which include Technology Operations and Concepts, Digital Citizenship, Research and Information Fluency, Communication and Collaboration, Critical Thinking, Problem Solving, and Decision Making. Each of these strands also has grade-level requirements. In addition, I consulted the National Educational Technology Standards (NETS) and the Performance Indicators for Students of the International Society for Technology in Education (ISTE 2007).

These larger goals of learning continue to shape my instruction and assessment. But student interest is the new objective that applied technology helped me to incorporate into my framework. When students are excited about a topic or are eager to develop a new skill, their motivation for learning accelerates. As the teacher, I am still in charge of guiding the educational journey in my classroom, but my students are not just passengers on the vehicle. Now they are deeply involved in setting the course of every learning adventure.

E-pals Enlarged

Many students arrive in the classroom each year with the idea that school computers are toys. They consider computer work as playtime, brief sessions during which they complete drills, surf the Internet, or try to play a video game while the teacher isn't looking. I wanted to begin the new school year by changing students' preconceived ideas about technology. At the same time, I hoped to build on their enthusiasm for new media and start my parallel learning journey with twenty-first-century tools.

Although word processing may not seem like an exciting "bells and whistles" application, it can improve students' abilities to get better-paying jobs and help them create, communicate, and collaborate. It is a nonthreatening tool that most teachers use daily. So my students and I mixed this plain-vanilla technology with another familiar ingredient, letter writing, and then blended in a digital version of brainstorming and digital photography to create a delicious new dish that had students begging for more.

For several years, my students had exchanged letters via snail mail with their peers in classrooms led by teachers I knew from professional conferences or through mutual acquaintances. (See Box 1.1 for tips about forming good distance partnerships.) Students enjoyed getting to know someone from outside the community, and the contacts with these peers from other classrooms also gave them an authentic reason to write. Because students realized that other adolescents would read their writing, they always took the activity seriously, and it

---

Box 1.1 | **Selecting a Writing Partner**

When searching for a teaching partner for a distance learning project, carefully consider your needs and those of your students. Ask yourself these questions:

- What is my vision, and does the other teacher(s) share it? What does the potential partner hope to gain from working with us?
- What is my time frame? Will this be a one-time project with a set deadline or an ongoing initiative?
- How does my partner feel about deadlines and corresponding in a timely manner? Will he or she communicate chiefly through e-mail or phone calls? How much time is my potential partner willing to devote to the project?
- What is my potential partner's experience with technology? Is he or she willing to learn and apply new applications for collaborative projects?
- What are the technology limitations or restrictions in my potential partner's classroom, school, or district?

- What kind of guidelines does my potential partner have regarding student privacy, safety, or posting student work?

By answering these questions before committing to a partnership, you will alleviate some of the frustrations and challenges of long-distance collaborations. However, if you've already formed a partnership and later discover that it's not a comfortable fit, you can still learn from the experience. For example, if the partner doesn't honor deadlines, you can guide your students to a conversation about work ethic and the consequences of their choices on others. When students find solutions to problems, they address ISTE's NETS for Students, especially Standard 4: Critical Thinking, Problem Solving, and Decision Making. Consider it on-the-job training.

became more meaningful to them than responding to a test prompt or a homework assignment.

With access to technology, their pen pals evolved into electronic pen pals, or e-pals. (There is a company named E-pals that connects students from around the world, but we are not affiliated with them.) They began exchanging their letters electronically instead of by snail mail.

Nice though it was, the letter exchange was still just an activity. I decided to enrich it by getting students to communicate with peers throughout the school year in multimedia formats that would enable them to develop their writing and editing skills in context. Because students were very motivated to write to their e-pals, I emphasized the importance of communicating with a specific audience in mind, focusing on rich content and sound mechanics while applying the practical use of technology—in this case, Microsoft Word and digital photography.

Grammar usage and mechanics are a major goal for improvement in our school and school district. The district requires language arts teachers to focus on mode (not genre) and gives us a weekly pacing guide for most subjects. In fifth grade, teachers are supposed to cover narrative, descriptive, and expository modes by the testing period in February. When I turn in my lesson plans, I must list the objectives supporting the district pacing guides. However, I also teach genre (types of writing, such as poetry, historical fiction, opinion/editorial pieces, and public service announcements) through each mode. The first week of school, we always begin by reading a high-interest novel (in this case, *Frindle* by Andrew Clements [1998]) that extends our conversations about the craft of writing.

Using the book as an example, I help students identify the reasoning behind the mechanics that enable them to express their thoughts. I give them a graphic organizer with the acronym COPS on it (see Box 1.2). As we read and discuss the book, we also have discussions concerning the basics of using COPS (capitalization, organization, punctuation, and spelling).

For example, when we see the end punctuation on a page, I ask students why the author has put the marks there.

"They are there because that's the end of a thought," a student says.

"What would happen if we didn't have any punctuation?" I ask.

Another student replies, "Well, it would just be mass confusion. You wouldn't be able to understand what was written at all."

Students take notes on the COPS editing tool to remind them not only of the rules of grammar and mechanics but also of the reasoning behind those rules. They see the relevance because those conclusions are drawn by them, not dictated by me. They own those answers.

Box 1.2 **A Tool for Editing**

Using the COPS (capitalization, organization, punctuation, and spelling) graphic organizer, students have to justify why a particular rule of grammar exists. They take notes as we practice using each rule. This graphic organizer becomes a tool that they keep in the front of their writing binders. At the beginning of the school year, they pull the sheet out while they are editing their own writing or editing a peer's writing. However, as the year progresses they usually commit the procedures to memory and don't need to check the graphic organizer very often. Students add additional items to the sheet that they think will be helpful to them while writing or editing. Figure 1.1 is a sample of one student's annotated COPS.

FIGURE 1.1

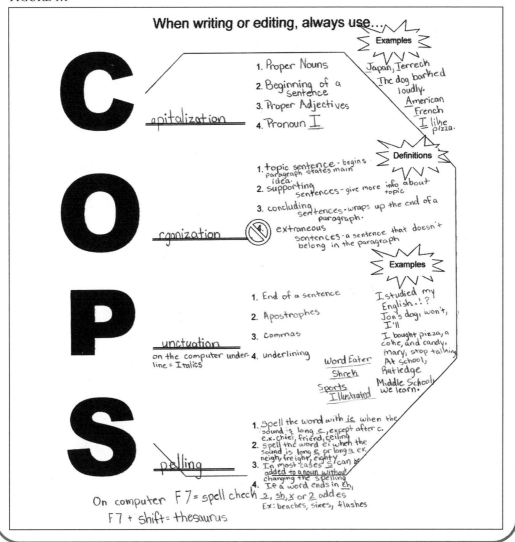

Why Do We Write?

When I introduce the idea of writing letters to students in another state, I ask my students, "What are some important things that we need to keep in mind if we are communicating with someone through our writing?"

For the most part they offer routine, concrete answers, such as, "We need to indent our paragraphs." I decide to challenge their assumptions so they can see the greater purpose of writing and not merely a set of rules to memorize.

Going Beyond Type and Send

With an Internet connection and a computer or smart phone, students today can communicate with anyone in the world on any topic. And they can get responses almost immediately, making reading and writing both personal and relevant. Text, photos, images, speech, movies, performances—an endless variety of new ways to share information has changed the way children learn.

As teachers, we should seize the chance to expand students' knowledge using the range of media and technology tools available. At the same time, we must ensure that students know how to do more than just "type and send."

How do we write so that the receiver understands our message? That's a central question for effective communication and a crucial lesson for students involved in a global exchange of information. Adolescents are egocentric and typically need help thinking about "the other." In writing, this connection translates into a consideration of audience and purpose.

"Does anyone know why we should indent paragraphs?" I ask.

"Because that's what the rule says," one brave soul ventures.

"Why does the rule say that?" I ask.

A mass of blank stares and furrowed brows greet my gaze. I can tell they are trying to find the answer they think I want to hear. Some of them break eye contact with me because they fear I will call on them and they won't know the right response. One student mentions that his previous teacher had taught him that he should always indent when writing paragraphs.

I ask, "Where else did you learn that or see that rule?"

Another student raises her hand to respond. "I saw it in a book I was reading," she says.

I ask her to explain what she notices about the indentations.

"Well," she says, "in my book you see that there are new paragraphs when characters are having a conversation. It changes whenever a different character speaks."

Another student adds, "You also indent for the new paragraph because it's a different thought."

I start to see clarity come into the faces of students as they move from confusion to "aha." I probe a bit further. "Why do you think looking at other writing is a good idea to understand what we are writing?"

After some thought, Jordan responds. "They are professional writers. They get paid to write. So if we write like them, we will become good writers too."

In addition to touching on grammar and mechanics, we identify different modes of writing by reading our book together. Using a descriptive passage, for example, students talk about being able to "see what the author is saying." We have a rich conversation about using language to visualize details.

The students begin compiling a list of characteristics of good writing, including some general ideas about craft and some ideas specific to the three different modes of writing that we study in fifth grade. As we continue reading *Frindle*, I help students identify other examples of descriptive writing (the mode that they scored lowest on in previous years) and to compare and contrast various passages.

Just as we learn from excellent writing, we can also learn from poor writing. I next guide my students through the same process looking at examples of e-pal letters previously written (with the student's permission and with all names removed). By using a document camera and the notation functions of an interactive whiteboard, students can identify errors, make changes, and justify those same changes, whether related to craft or mechanics. The changes serve as a reminder of the importance of communicating effectively through writing.

Technology Makes Mundane Tasks Fun

In the past when we made the list of characteristics of good writing or brainstormed ideas, students would write their thoughts on pieces of paper and then we would share these as a whole group, compiling a list on chart paper or the interactive whiteboard. Both of these methods had drawbacks. Often the lists were messy, making them difficult to read. Sometimes students might want to refer to the lists at home but had either left them in the classroom or didn't have time to copy the information before the end of the period. Other times we needed to use the whiteboard for another purpose and the list would get lost between classes.

Then I discovered a tool called Wallwisher (www.wallwisher.com). This free interface enables users to create a digital brainstorming wall and then leave comments through virtual yellow "sticky notes." The notes can include typed ideas (limited to 160 characters), Web links, videos, and photos, among other things. You can set Wallwisher's sharing and viewing capabilities to be public or private. In the latter case, you share the specific URL only with those you want to view the information.

Wallwisher is deceptively simple. Students can comment on topics individually or in groups, in class or at home, and as a teacher you can respond directly to the comments as well. You and your students can also move the sticky notes around, regrouping ideas and reorganizing categories as the discussion matures. The best part is that the changes save automatically and perpetually, giving students access to the information throughout the school year in whatever setting they choose.

I like to show my students how to use Wallwisher collectively and then let them work in small groups to refine their ideas. Multiple users can be active on the same wall at the same time. Then as an entire class we can review the changes and organize the thoughts.

As the budding writers were brainstorming their lists of characteristics of good e-pal letters, for example, I traveled from group to group, listening to their conversations. (See Box 1.3 to learn more about building collaborative teamwork within the classroom.) I found that many groups went right back to

---

Box 1.3 | Collaborative Teamwork within the Classroom

In addition to helping my students become better writers with the aid of technology, I wanted to create a more collaborative environment that would teach them how to work together effectively (see NETS for Students 2, Communication and Collaboration, and 5, Digital Citizenship). Before school begins each year, I now look at a student's standardized test scores, exceptionalities, physical considerations, behavior records, reading levels, and any other data that I can gather. Most of this information is provided to the homeroom teachers at our school on a student information card. I don't pigeonhole a student but identify strengths and weaknesses that I can use when determining learning groups and leadership roles. I place students in different groups throughout the year, depending on the needs and circumstances.

For use within each group, I have designed jobs that help students nurture various skills.

These jobs rotate each week so that students get to handle the full range of responsibilities in a collaborative learning team. One job is the director, who is responsible for leading the team, solving disputes, and keeping team members on-task during discussions and activities. The groups also have a recorder, who keeps track of written materials and notes. The group's reporter is responsible for speaking for the group, which fosters public communication skills. Finally, each group has a gopher, a person who ensures that the team members have all the materials they need for the day's activities and then puts these materials back at the end of class. The gophers focus on organization, time management, and planning skills. Students get so involved in their groups that they create team names and logos to demonstrate their pride and affiliation.

listing the grammar rules and seemed surprised when I asked them to justify their answers: "Why do we need to have five paragraphs?" "Why do we need to describe our school?" I had to assure them that their ideas weren't wrong, but that I merely wanted to understand why they had included an item on the list.

After about twenty minutes of small-group brainstorming time, I asked students to share their ideas with the whole class, but they had to justify their thinking. As I scribed their ideas on Wallwisher, I saw them shaking their heads in agreement or disagreement about what was listed. Spontaneous discussions emerged, and students started asking each other to explain their thinking.

"Do we all have to agree with the same ideas?" I asked them.

When I didn't get an immediate response, I tried a different approach. I asked Elizabeth, "What is your favorite color?"

She answered, "My favorite color is baby blue." I told her that my favorite color was green.

Then I asked the class, "Do Elizabeth and I have to agree on the same favorite color?"

"Of course not," they replied.

So I asked, "Then do we have to all agree on what to include in our first e-pal letter?"

Those lovely lightbulbs started sparking again. Luna commented, "We don't all have to agree, but some things will have to be the same, like the grammar rules and some of the stuff we write about. The other students will need to be able to know about us from our writing."

At this stage in the process, I could see that they were beginning to tie together the personal relevance of the technology tools to enhance their own writing in their own voice. Reflecting later, I wondered why I had been reluctant to probe their thinking in this manner before. I realized that I had seldom asked them to justify their answers because I couldn't predict the outcome. As teachers, we never know what will come out of a student's mouth. With trepidation, I asked the first few "whys" fearing that my students would give an answer that I couldn't weave back into a learning opportunity. But their excitement was so contagious, it actually spurred me on to ask more "whys" and to let go of my fear that I wouldn't have the ability to guide the learning curve. Each breakthrough became a reason to celebrate or a new path to discover, not a reason to panic.

Our First Writing Rubric

One of the first things that other teachers, administrators, and parents want to know is how you will assess the writing activities supported and created with technology. I know that when I was first given the task to prepare students for the state writing assessment, I was completely overwhelmed. After researching, attending workshops, and fumbling around through trial and error, I devised a basic rubric that I thought scored student work similarly to the state writing rubric. However, I noticed that often students wrote what they wanted without paying attention to the rubric.

Resolved to achieve better cooperation and results, I decided to guide my students in forming their own rubric for their first e-pal letter. We returned to the lists of characteristics of good writing that each team had created, and after the representatives from each team had justified the importance of the various items, we sorted the lists into categories. Wallwisher made this process easy. Four major categories emerged: description of self, explanation of school/class, editing, and digital publication. Note: The specific items and categories change from letter to letter and project to project. However, content, grammar, mechanics, mode, and project publication are included in each of the projects. Box 1.4 provides examples of some of our rubrics.

I know that many teachers feel uncomfortable stepping into the territory of making rubrics. When I first began using rubrics, I searched online to get an idea of how other educators assessed their students in their writing and in projects. One popular site is Rubistar (http://rubistar.4teachers.org/index.php). I did find some really well-made samples at some of these sites. However, once I shifted the focus and decision making over to the students (with my guidance), the rubric seemed to mean much more to them when they were making it than when I gave them a ready-made sample. By giving the learners a rubric, I was taking away their power to guide the decisions throughout the process. The students should always be the center of the choices; it's their writing, their project, their learning path.

As students began writing their first letters, I moved from group to group to observe the process and their interactions. I guided the students in identifying the different modes of writing within their letters as well as good writing practices and referred to the examples that we had read previously. If I saw a pattern of error, I took a couple of minutes to teach a quick lesson.

For example, when I got to Jordan, I pointed to several lowercase letters and asked, "What do these letters have in common?"

He didn't respond right away, so I tried another approach. "Read these words for me, please," I said, pointing to *fultondale elementary school, fultondale, birmingham,* and *central avenue.*

He read the words out loud, and then I asked, "What are all of those words?"

"Oh, they're all names," he said, after thinking for a moment or two. "Should they all have capital letters?"

Box 1.4	**Student-Created Rubrics**

Figure 1.2 is an example of how the students score one another on a scale of 0 to 4 (4 being the highest). This parallels the scoring system for our standardized writing assessment. At this point in the year, I am the only one formally assessing their writing for a grade. Students use their rubric to share comments and give feedback throughout the process.

Figure 1.3 is a rubric that I created on Microsoft Word and use to evaluate students' progress from one writing assignment to the next. The categories on this rubric have been selected by students. When I assess students' writing for a final grade at the end of each project, I add a grade point value for each of the categories. If the number of categories isn't evenly divided by 100,

the students decide the maximum point value for each category.

When students come to conference with me, we look at the letter together and discuss the patterns that I found. I have the students locate the errors in their writing and explain how they could improve in future writing.

In the last column, students set their goals for future writing projects. They write their goals in their writing folders so that they can refer to them when they begin the next writing assignment.

This is the basic format I use for all of the rubrics the students create for any writing project. Of course, the categories adjust to meet the needs of the students or to fit the type of project in which they are engaged.

FIGURE 1.2   *(continued)*

| Box 1.4 | **Student-Created Rubrics** *(continued)* |

E-pal Grades—August

Author's Note: In the Teacher's Comments, I made notes that serve as a reminder of what I need to discuss with a student when we conference and set individual goals. I use these records to note a student's weaknesses or strengths and chart his or her progress throughout the school year.

Student	Description of Self (25 points)	Explanation of School/ Class (25 points)	Editing Using COPS (25 points)	Digital (25 points)	Teacher's Comments	Student's Personal Goals
Elise	20 points	20 points	15 points	25 points	Great content; leaves words out of sentences (80%)	Edit more carefully to be sure words aren't left out
Juan Carlos	25 points	20 points	10 points	25 points	Proper nouns; spelling; homophones (80%)	Capitalize proper nouns
Addy	15 points	15 points	10 points	20 points	Sentence end punctuation; think of audience when explaining or describing (60%)	Remember audience; double check for end punctuation
Quinn	20 points	20 points	15 points	25 points	Paragraphs need to have more information in them; edit carefully (80%)	Add more details; check writing more carefully
Oliver	20 points	20 points	10 points	25 points	Homophones; needs interesting sentence construction; possessives (75%)	Try building different types of sentences; use possessives correctly
Ricky	20 points	20 points	25 points	25 points	Develops paragraphs with several supporting sentences (90%)	Add details to make it more interesting
Elisha	25 points	25 points	15 points	25 points	Run-on sentences; nice description of self (90%)	Use proper punctuation with sentences

FIGURE 1.3

"What do you think?" I asked, putting the responsibility on him.

"Yes, they should have capital letters because they are proper nouns. Just like in the book we were reading and the notes we took on our COPS sheet."

Traveling around the classroom and having these short conferences, I could catch many of the errors that students were making while they were in the process of composing their letters. Through these one-on-one conversations, I guided them to take responsibility for assessing their own writing while keeping in mind the rubric they had created.

Collaborative Editing

As students completed their first drafts, they chose two peers to edit their writing. The editors often pulled out the COPS graphic organizer and the rubric to help them suggest revisions.

"Elizabeth, this doesn't make sense to me," Rachel said to her partner at one point.

"But it makes sense to me," Elizabeth responded.

"Okay, I guess it's just me," Rachel said, backing off hesitantly.

When I heard this exchange, I realized that there were several omissions in Elizabeth's letter about an upcoming quinceañera, a coming-of-age ceremony for girls that is celebrated in many Latin American cultures. I asked Rachel, "Can you tell Elizabeth what exactly doesn't make sense?"

"I'm not really able to understand what this party is all about and why you are practicing for it for weeks," Rachel said.

"Oh," Elizabeth said thoughtfully. "Well, a quinceañera is like a girl's sweet sixteen birthday, but in Mexico we celebrate your fifteenth birthday. There is a church service and a big party with specific dances you do. It's a lot like a wedding."

"So, Elizabeth," I asked, "why do you think Rachel was confused?"

"Because I didn't really explain it all that well?" she responded. "Maybe I should add more details. Oh, like those seeing words we saw in our book."

As this conversation shows, students don't typically want to criticize one another, especially early in the school year. Usually they will give back a letter with very little changed and few comments. They need nudging, as I nudged Rachel, until they get comfortable giving more substantive feedback. After students receive two edits from peers, they go to the computer and type their letters using Microsoft Word.

At first, I asked peer editors to only mark edits on the paper, explain their suggestions, and move on. But after some contemplation and observation, I noticed that my students were rushing through the editing of one another's writing so they could get to the computer to work on their own letters. Consequently, I had the students fill out a rubric for each letter they reviewed. They kept all of their drafts and rubrics from peers in their writing folders. While assessing their writing, I would go back and look at the original or the peers' comments, if necessary, to see who had read/edited/scored the writing. In this way, I could locate any weaknesses in the editing that I would need to address later during a small-group lesson. Having students give feedback to peers also reinforced the idea that this was their rubric, not mine. They were being scored based on their decisions during the creation of the rubric.

Project Assessment

To evaluate my students' final writing, I used their rubrics. I made comments under each category and then met one-on-one with each student to discuss the writing. I asked the students to explain their choices and set goals for their next writing project.

As the year progressed, these rubrics and goals established a record of each student's progress. It also served as a way for me to differentiate instruction as needed through one-on-one, whole-group, or small-group instruction. The students focused not on grades, although their writing was assessed, but on their growth. After the first couple of writing activities, students rarely asked what their grade was on a particular assignment.

At the beginning of the year, I was tempted to skip the individual, goal-setting conferences from time to time due to the constraints of my schedule and district-mandated pacing guides. However, my students would begin asking me when they would be talking with me about their writing. They actually kept *me* on-task with their assessment, showing me how important these conferences were to them. By the middle of the year, our one-on-one conferencing sessions lasted about twenty to twenty-five minutes total per writing activity. The students usually had a clear view of where they were headed with their writing and why. Of course, I also knew where they needed to be by the end of the school year, so I was able to guide them appropriately.

Extending Our Learning Tools

While watching my students type their first e-pal letters, I realized that most of them routinely used text lingo to communicate on cell phones and e-mail, but they had not had been formally trained to use computer keyboards. Since that text lingo crept into the correspondence, I knew that I needed to teach them a basic lesson on how to type on a word processor (reinforcing NETS for Students 6, Technology Operations and Concepts). I created a presentation on typing and using a word processor and then demonstrated these basic rules. Then I placed a reminder card on top of each of our classroom computers that students could refer to as they continued practicing throughout the year.

At this point you may be wondering why the students were not writing directly to their e-pals through e-mail. This particular year our e-pal project involved two schools in different states. To meet the safety restrictions of both schools, my teaching partner and I had our students write their letters on a word processor and then save the files to flash drives before we, the teachers, sent them as e-mail attachments. Although this process was more time-consuming than letting students send their letters directly by e-mail, it gave us more control. For the safety of my students, I read everything before it left or entered my classroom.

In addition to focusing on typing, I taught a basic lesson about digital photography because the students wanted to include a photo of themselves with their writing. Most nonfiction writing includes photos, charts, maps, or diagrams, they reasoned, so why shouldn't their writing use similar images? I brought an old digital camera from home, and the students used it to take photos of each other. (See Box 1.5 for tips about digital photography.) They

---

| Box 1.5 | **Students' Digital Photography Tips** |

Each year, before setting my students loose with a digital camera, I take a few minutes to go over some basic photography tips. When I first used digital photography in the classroom, I often noticed that students would take photos in which the subjects appeared very small, out of focus, and drastically off-center. I created a simple presentation of photographs and asked students to identify what they liked or disliked about the photos, such as good and bad examples of framing, lighting, and background selection. Over the years, students added photography tips to my original list.

Here is a list of some of the tips my students compiled. These tips apply to taking realistic photographs of people and places. Students get to create artistic photos at other times for other purposes.

- Fill up the screen with the subject of the photo. If you are taking a photo of a person, the person, not the wall or ceiling behind him or her, should fill up most of the photo.

- Look at the background behind the subject you are photographing. People generally don't want the appearance of branches growing out of their heads or cars driving into their ears.

- Be aware of the lighting and shadows. If you are within five feet of your subject and it's dark outside, chances are the flash won't illuminate for a photo. Be careful not to place the subject where shadows or light cut across a subject's face.

- Be willing to move to a different height to get the best shot of the subject.

More great digital photography tips can be found on the Kodak Web site (www.kodak.com) under the tab Tips & Projects Exchange. Kodak's "Learn" page covers the basics that students need to know for this type of photography.

attached the camera's memory card to our classroom computer and inserted the images into their letters.

When I first tried to send the e-pal letters and photos, the files were too large to go through the other school's server. Frustration set in as my students watched me try and fail several times. Later, after consulting some friends, I figured out the difference in the meaning of "size" in relation to digital photography. Although the students had changed the physical space that the photos took up on their letters, they had not changed the pixel count of the actual photos. At home that night, I used a simple photo-editing program, Photo Suite, to figure out how to resize the photos. I shared the process with my students the following day.

As they continued to write throughout the school year, my students often wanted to share their work with their e-pals. They became more thoughtful and focused to ensure that they could effectively explain the correct steps in a project or communicate new information. Boxes 1.6, 1.7, and 1.8 provide descriptions and examples of their later projects. Often their e-pals would write

---

Box 1.6	**Scanner Collage Book Reports**

Students select a book of interest, read the book, and write a list of ten to fifteen items that represent different aspects of that book. For example, if a student read *Harry Potter and the Sorcerer's Stone*, a wand might be on the list, with an explanation about the role of the wand in the book.

On an assigned day, students bring in the ten to fifteen items on their lists. I encourage the students to be creative and to collect small items they already have, can borrow, or create themselves. They place these items face down on the scanner, cover the back with a piece of fabric (because the scanner lid won't close fully), scan, and then print. (A sample is shown in Figure 1.4.)

The students are always amazed at the depth and dimension of their colorful projects. They also have assisted younger students in creating Valentine's Day and Mother's Day collages. Many students have come back and asked to use the scanner to create collages for project covers and birthday cards for relatives. Another teacher, not having a scanner, let her students create the collages and take a digital photo of them.

This is a very simple project for students to complete. Once a student finishes, he or she can assist the next student.

This is also an easy first project to explain to their e-pals. These days, we still create scanner collages, but instead of printing them we upload them to our class Web site.

FIGURE 1.4 One Student's Scanner Collage

back and share things that they had done as well. In this way, we created a distance learning community in which the students taught each other not only the content that they shared through their writing but also the technology projects and applications that they were learning in the classroom. Students took notes, asked good questions, and adopted technology more quickly because they had to understand the applications before passing the information along in their next correspondence.

Box 1.7 **READ Posters**

Students select a book of interest, read it, and then retell the story from a character's point of view. This project reinforces summarizing, understanding point of view, creativity, and creating digital photography.

On the due date, students bring in their books, costumes, and backdrops, such as a fabric remnant that relates to the setting of the book. Once again, I encourage students to create their costumes from things they own or can borrow.

Students then take photos of each other in costume in front of their backdrops and holding their books, similar to the celebrity posters that the American Library Association produces to promote reading (see Figures 1.5 and 1.6). They attach the camera's memory card to the computer and use the photo editing software that comes with the camera to add the word *READ* to their image before printing.

FIGURE 1.5

FIGURE 1.6

Box 1.8 | Digital Quilt Blocks

Our e-pals shared this project with us. Using Microsoft Publisher, they created quilt blocks that illustrated their unique personal qualities and interests. My students wanted to make similar quilt blocks where each block would represent a different learner, but we did not have the right software. So I asked my students if they had any ideas. Sean spoke up and said, "Why can't we create scanner collages that represent each of us? Then we could send the collages to our e-pals."

What a wonderful, simple, and inexpensive solution! Because my students already knew how to use the scanner, they were able to manage this project on their own, mostly before the regular school day started.

When the final quilt was assembled (see Figure 1.7), the students started noticing similarities in one another's blocks. Throughout the quilt project, students were able to make connections with students other than the one with whom they were corresponding. They would talk to their classroom peers and ask them to include a message to their e-pals about common interests, such as playing soccer. The quilt was a representation of their evolving digital-learning community. More recently, my students suggested that we create a digital friendship quilt and display it on our class Web site.

FIGURE 1.7 The Students' Scanner Collage Quilt

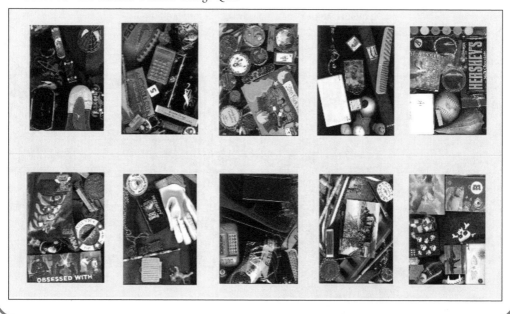

Technology-Enhanced Learning That Lasts

In the years since our first e-pal experiments, we have moved beyond basic letter writing to collaborating through a safe and secure, adjustable learning environment called Moodle (http://moodle.org). A free, open-source network, Moodle can be downloaded to a server and made available to anyone who is given access to it. Moodle was made available for free to educators in Indiana by the Rose-Hulman Institute of Technology in Terre Haute, Indiana. The two Indiana teachers with whom we partnered contacted university officials, and they graciously agreed to make Moodle available for all of the students working on our collaborative projects. Students uploaded photos, used the discussion boards, participated in chat room discussions, and created wikis together, all in this protected environment. (For more about publishing student work and Internet safety, see Box 1.9.)

Through this platform my students have the opportunity to discuss ideas with other learners across the country in a much more up-to-the-minute mode. In the past, before I used technology tools, we would only be able to

---

| Box 1.9 | **Publishing Students' Work and Internet Safety** |

Because many of my students have parents serving in the military overseas or do not live with both of their parents, I want to ensure that they have the opportunity to share their writing, no matter the distance. Technology tools provide a perfect solution to this challenge. I built a very simple Web site (http://ramsaysclass.com) and use it to post my students' projects, photos, accomplishments, and classroom news and updates. This broadened the audience for which they were writing, while strengthening the connection between home and school.

I chose to build a Web site and obtain a private domain for a nominal price, but there are other free venues available, such as Google's Blogger (www.blogger.com), edublogs (http://edublogs.org/), and Weebly (www.weebly.com). Today many districts provide server space for each teacher. Blogs and wikis (see Chapter 6) are also free and easy to use. Many of them come with built-in security features.

When students register at our school, their parents sign a basic media release form. However, to further ensure the children's safety, we use only first names to identify online writing. We also change personal information. My students refer to their "secret identities," which serves as a springboard for discussions about Internet safety and digital citizenship.

A good resource for teaching online "netiquette" is *Net Cetera: Chatting with Kids About Being Online*, a free publication from the Federal Trade Commission (2010) found at www.onguardonline.gov/pdf/tec04.pdf. We read and discuss this publication in class, and then the students take it home to share with their parents. While discussing Internet safety, I have the students explain the importance of each of the safety precautions, making it a personally relevant lesson.

write three e-pal letters a year through postal mail. Using e-mail attachments, we could usually have six correspondences in a school year. With Moodle, we can have several correspondences a day from school or home. All of the students can be online at the same time, responding to questions, asking questions, telling about a recent event in their lives, or brainstorming about an upcoming project.

Whether my learners are reading a letter they received from their e-pals or a response on Moodle, I often get spontaneous comments such as this one: "Hey, Mrs. Ramsay, they are reading *Island of the Blue Dolphins* like us. He said he thought the book was boring and I told him exactly why it's an exciting book. They haven't done a squid dissection, so I'm going to tell them all about it."

Regardless of the communications method, my students are always eager to respond quickly to their learning partners, something that technology enables them to do. When I announce that it's time to stop and go to PE or lunch, they often say, "Aw, do we have to? Can we skip lunch and keep writing?"

As I reflect on this, I wonder what has changed. I've taught writing before. I've had projects with technology before. I've had learning teams before. So what's different? It is this: Students no longer view writing as assignments directed by me. They are the ones in control, engaged in meaningful work enhanced by technology.

CHAPTER

2

Poetry to Podcasts

Standards and Skills
- Collaboration
- Creativity
- Research and inquiry: habitats, biomes, ecosystems
- Poetry composition
- Self-assessment

Technology Tools
- Microsoft Word
- Lintor Make-A-Book (software and publishing materials)
- StoryJumper (www.storyjumper.com)

It's early one school morning. My students have settled into the class routine of unloading their backpacks, getting out their homework so I can grade it, and writing their new assignments into their agendas. As they begin their morning practice with editing and spelling, the inkjet printer in the back of the classroom sputters to life. The first responses to the e-pal letters have arrived!

When I alert the students, huge smiles spread across their faces and excited whispers spark across the classroom like a match on dry tinder. I pass out the responses to their letters, and spontaneous conversations break out.

"Hey," Felicia says, "my e-pal has a brother and a sister like me."

"Mine has been playing soccer as long as I have," Kevin declares.

"They don't have writing lab like we do, but they have an art class," another student announces.

The students automatically make comparisons between their lives and those of the peers they have never met until now, through their writing. This much I had expected from my previous experience with e-pal exchanges. But much to my surprise, this new pursuit goes well beyond a getting-to-know-you activity.

Looking back, I realize the significance of this moment. It signaled the power of digital communication to foster collaboration and creativity, not just for students but for teachers as well.

Seizing the Moment

I might not have encouraged my students to depend on one another to create, learn, and explore if I hadn't previously experienced the benefits of collaborating with my own peers. Shortly before I began the new, improved e-pal project, I had participated in several online, real-time webinars and presentations in a free, multiuser virtual environment called Second Life (http://secondlife.com). Meeting educators from around the world through these activities, I developed my own personal learning network (PLN), a modern-day version of a guild, where people can consult with and learn from expert craftsmen (see Box 2.1 for more).

Box 2.1 | Building Your Personal Learning Network (PLN)

Several years ago, while teaching the state-required ancient civilizations curriculum, I received a notice from my principal stating that at midyear, the grade-level curriculum had been rewritten and I was now required to teach American history, preparing students for the upcoming standardized tests covering that subject. Having no classroom resources or money to purchase any materials for my students, I went to the library and searched the Internet for information that could help me quickly convey the important themes and events so my students would have a reasonable chance of success on the test. After many hours of solitary research, I developed some tools and tracked down useful resources for my students.

Now here I was several years later trying to learn something new that would once again help my students excel. However, this time I was able to use the Internet to connect with other educators who were also searching for effective ways to reach their twenty-first-century learners. We shared ideas, experiences, resources, and tips. Colleagues from around the world became my twenty-four-hour-a-day educator hotline.

In searching for quality professional development, I found a webinar series offered by ISTE. Webinars are appealing because you can get ideas and tools in a presentation format from anyone in the world in real time. In many cases, you can also view webinars that have been archived for use after the live presentations. All you need to

| Box 2.1 | **Building Your Personal Learning Network (PLN)** *(continued)* |

participate is a computer with Internet access and sound, a small investment of your time (an hour or so), and, possibly, a small monetary investment to the organization or person presenting.

The more webinars that I viewed, the more people I was able to connect with on Nings (networking Web sites), blogs, Second Life, and Twitter. Each of these tools helped me find people with common interests with whom I could speak, ask questions, vent frustrations, and celebrate successes. In Second Life, topics are advertised by different groups of teachers affiliated with organizations such as ISTE or Discovery Educators Network (DEN). Most often there is no registration, fee, or preparation required to attend a session. You download the Second Life viewers free of charge. To attend a presentation, discussion, or workshop, you just sign into Second Life at the designated time and meet at the designated location within the virtual environment, as the sessions are conducted synchronously.

In Second Life, as I attended presentations, I discovered that there was a valuable backchat dialogue where the attendees could discuss the topics being presented. At first, I was hesitant to comment in this way. But soon I was adding my own comments and asking questions of the other educators participating. It was the closest thing I had found to participating in a live conference and interacting with educators without having to travel from my home.

These experiences led me to Twitter; many of the people who conducted webinars or who were in Second Life posted "tweets" regularly. I was often asked by other educators for my Twitter name, so I thought I needed to investigate it. Twitter is a micro-blogging site that limits posts to 140 characters. To set up a free account, you register an e-mail address on the Twitter Web site. It's easy to search and follow other people's posts. I

started with people whom I had heard during workshops or webinars. When searching for people or groups to track, you can read the most recent posts to get a sense of the value of the posts. Click on the Follow button to add the person or group to your list. It's just as easy to select Stop Following to later remove them from your Twitter feed. When you find someone from whom you learn a lot, you can also see who they follow, and add them to your Twitter feed.

Twitter was appealing because while I might not have the time to write a blog entry or review many blogs in a week, I could read short posts quickly and easily. Twitter became a quick professional resource that I could access at any time during the day. Often my students would dream up a project to support their writing, not knowing whether there was a Web 2.0 tool to help. Instead of spending hours searching for information myself, I could tweet about it, and within a few minutes (or sometimes a few hours), I would have plenty of suggestions.

It was so exciting to realize I wasn't alone trying out new teaching practices. I now had connections with other educators who could give me advice about what had worked for them and how they had overcome similar challenges. Because the information online is overwhelming in size and scope, it's reassuring to have a team, or PLN, working with you to simplify and summarize. With my newfound network, I can find just about anything that I need for my students in a matter of minutes.

Networking sites, such as The Educator's PLN (http://edupln.com/), help you find and connect with other teachers. Once you find someone who contributes ideas that you find valuable, you can continue tracking them on blogs, Twitter, and Second Life, ever widening your own PLN.

With the positive results from my PLN, I seized the chance to help my students learn as I had—by picking other people's brains. In the first letters that my students wrote to their e-pals, they included information about our classroom. Many of them mentioned that we were reading *Island of the Blue Dolphins* by Scott O'Dell. It turned out that their e-pals had also read that novel and had visited Channel Islands National Park, the real-life setting for the novel. They mailed us a poster of the habitat on the real island of the blue dolphins and shared interesting facts about sea animals. My students love learning interesting trivia about many subjects, but they are particularly fascinated with animals, so the details in the e-pal letters proved irresistible.

As they continued sharing details from their e-pals letters with their classmates, my students created a spontaneous lesson on habitats and literature. Two students asked if they could Google the animal mentioned in their letters to see what it looked like. As they did, other students crowded around the computer, eager to get a better view of the discoveries.

I was amazed at their response. In the past, when I had tried to engage my students in a discussion about the animal habitats described in *Island of the Blue Dolphins*, I had never gotten this kind of reaction or enthusiasm. I had worked hard to make my lessons interesting, using hands-on samples taken from a local sea lab, photographs, and a substantial collection of fictional and nonfictional picture books. What was so different this time around? Instead of the teacher who stood before them every day of the school year, they could now learn from new age-mate friends on the other side of the country and augment that knowledge through immediate Internet access.

Okay, I'm admitting some naiveté, but this was such an eye-opening experience for me. Not only was I discovering the power of collaborative learning through my own peer-to-peer exchanges (see Box 2.1), but also I was realizing the impact of students teaching other students, assisted by technology. Through this simple letter exchange, my students gained a much deeper understanding of animal habitats, as well as the role that the environment played in the novel we were reading. I wanted to harness this enthusiasm for learning, which came from other students, not me.

Deeper Reflection

In previous years, I would have had students share the interesting tidbits from their letters and write responses before we moved on with our regular lessons. This time, having seen the enthusiasm build from personal connections and networked information, I decided to draw out the conversation and guide them toward deeper reflection.

My students acknowledged that they had stereotyped their e-pals before knowing them, based on the region of the country they were from. They discovered from the personal letters how much they were alike. Because their e-pals had shared so much information about their home state of Arizona, my students became curious about researching Alabama's history so they could include some details in their next letters. They also repeatedly commented on how much they had learned about science and the historical and scientific accuracies in *Island of the Blue Dolphins* from reading the e-pal exchanges. Over and over, I heard, "I never knew that . . ."

I didn't want this zeal to fade away. I noticed that many of my students had started taking notes about what they had learned so they could include more details in their responses. They were itching to write back immediately, but I wanted to ensure that they went beyond strictly listing facts. After I mentioned this goal to my students, I gave them time to think about how they might communicate their new knowledge of marine life to their new friends in a more creative and expansive way.

Ashlyn, drawing on her previous experiences, spoke up first: "We could draw a picture or make a poster."

"True," I responded. "I wonder if there might be some additional ideas of ways to present the same information."

I pushed myself to wait, remembering the enthusiasm sparked by their earlier conversations, when they were not concerned about providing the right answer to the teacher's prompt.

"Maybe we could write a book of what we want to share with them and include the photos we just found online, including some of Ashlyn's ideas," Luna suggested.

"Another good idea," I said, pausing again to let them think about each other's comments.

"Wait," Nick interrupted. "How would they get these books? We would have to mail them and it would take a longer time than if we e-mailed something to them."

"Not if we posted them on our Web site," Sean said. "What if instead of each of us making a book, we make one book together? We could post it on our Web site, but also make one book to mail to them the old-fashioned way."

"Yeah," Nick said, "that could work."

"Okay, what kind of writing do you think should be in this book?" I asked.

Several students named different genres, and then Sean spoke up: "What if we write poetry? It can include a bit of everything—what we've learned from our letters, the new things we've learned, and photographs."

A chorus of voices agreed to this idea; they were ready to get started. As I guided this discussion, in the back of my mind I was thinking, *Did I really just let my students choose their next writing assignment? Did I just hand the reins over to them?* Yes, I did.

The next question I asked myself was how technology might support their ideas. Once again, my students had already begun answering that question for me. They wanted to publish the poems on our class Web site, which meant they could use Microsoft Word to do the typing and save files to a flash drive. Then, once I got home, I could easily copy and paste the material into Microsoft FrontPage, the software I used to design our class Web site.

In addition, my students requested that we publish a hardbound book to mail to their e-pal class. In the past, I usually had my students publish their writing using products from Lintor Make-A-Book. When they shared their books at Young Authors Conferences, they were always proud of their final projects because the books looked so polished; they weren't cut and pasted into a prebound book or just stapled together. They usually would ask if they could go and show their work to former teachers or administrators.

Lintor Make-A-Book is not a free tool. However, once you purchase the publishing package, which includes software with all of the templates and the basic tools for binding your books, all you will have to do is replenish the covers. An accompanying video demonstrates how to complete the binding process.

I showed the students a sample book that my former students had made. They were very excited that, in their words, "it would look very professional" (see Box 2.2).

Today we are still publishing books using Lintor's products because my students love the final result. However, because we are now writing and creating constantly with not just one school but five other schools, I had to find an additional way for my students to publish books so their online collaborators would have access to their work.

After consulting with my PLN, I found StoryJumper, a free, child-centered Web site that enables authors to create and publish their own digital storybooks (see Box 2.3). My students can share their books with anyone by simply sending the URL. On my class Web site, I have links to each of the books so that their friends and families can also read the books from anywhere in the world. Also, for a fee, a parent can purchase a hardbound version of their young author's work.

Our classroom publishing ventures occur organically; I don't force them. I believe that teachers often think of technology tools as something extra to add

---

Box 2.2 **Publishing a Book: Combining Old-Fashioned and New Technology Tools**

Lintor Make-A-Book products can be found online at www.lintorpublishing.com/default.php. Whenever I bring examples of my students' work to workshops or presentations, other teachers always "ooh" and "ah" over the Lintor products. They are impressive to see. In the initial publishing package, you get the software, which gives you templates that open in simple word processing programs. The templates enable you to choose different sizes of books as well as a variety of front cover labels. You also get a site license, heavy-duty stapler and staples, thirty hardback book covers in the size that you choose, binding pages and reinforcement strips, and a video that explains the binding process.

Usually my students understand the binding process after I demonstrate it just once. It's a simple process with a "Wow!" ending.

Figure 2.1 shows a few of the poetry books that my students created for one year's Young Authors Conference. I wish I could show you some of the interior pages with the students' writing and artwork, but they treasured them so much that they took them home.

FIGURE 2.1 These poetry books were created using Lintor Make-A-Book.

---

to lessons instead of a way to shape learning. My experience with writing and publishing using online tools taught me to retune my ear and really listen to what my students were saying about how technology enriches their lives. By turning my attention to their world and climbing down from my omniscient teacher's perch, I was able to capture something that I had missed in the past— a deeper understanding of what makes today's students passionate to know more.

Box 2.3 | **Publishing a Digital Storybook**

StoryJumper can be found at www.storyjumper .com. The site includes many samples to read online. My students enjoy the animation and sound effects as you turn the pages. As Elizabeth said, "It's just like you're reading a real book." Of course, they *are* real books; they are just digital!

Before you can create a book on StoryJumper, you must set up a free account. You can "create a class" so each student can work on his or her own book, but I chose to supervise my students to meet safety standards. I sign in under my account, they create their book, and I sign out. Please be aware of the StoryJumper Children's Privacy Policy, which applies to all students under the age of thirteen. Our district also has a release form that parents must sign, giving permission for their children's work to be published digitally. Be

sure to know the requirements for your school and school district.

StoryJumper has an abundance of backgrounds, clipart, and textboxes from which a young author can choose. Also, students can upload their own artwork or photographs to include in their books.

Once students have completed their books, they have different options for publishing. They can publish just for the reader, just for friends and family, or for anyone. We usually make it public (available for anyone to read) because we have more than two hundred people reading our current books. They can see and read the books, but not edit them. And if a parent or someone else wants to purchase a hardbound version of the books, they can do that too.

Reaching Consensus About Assessment

Hoping that our first successful rubric-making experience wasn't a fluke, my student groups set out to brainstorm ideas about what should be included in each person's poem.

As I had done during their previous small-group discussions with their letters, I listened to their conversations, often prompting them to justify their choices. At one table, the students were engaged in an intense debate.

"I think we should each include some of the information that we learned from our letters," one student said.

"But I don't want to write about sea anemones," another student whined.

"It wouldn't be fair to your e-pal if you don't use the sea life information that she sent in her letter," the first student explained kindly. "It would probably make her mad."

A third student in the group interjected: "I think sea anemones are really cool. Why don't you like them?"

"I really like orca whales and I want to write a poem about orca whales," the defiant student said, noticeably pouting.

At this point I stepped in. "So what would be a solution that would meet everyone's wishes?"

Silent thoughts followed. My inner voice nagged me to take over and give them the solution, but from what I had witnessed earlier I knew it would mean more if the students found the solution themselves.

The third student ventured a compromise. "What if I write about the sea anemone and she writes about my animal, which is an orca whale?" he said.

"So, how will you reflect this in your list?" I asked.

"Maybe we can trade letters and share facts as long as all of the animals are included in a poem," the first student suggested. "Does that sound reasonable to everyone?"

They unanimously agreed.

Rubric Writing, Round Two

After all the groups had completed their brainstorming sessions, a representative from each shared the group's ideas about what should be included in the class poems. We followed the same process as we had with their letters, first making a master list and then organizing it into categories. I required students to justify their choices. As with the first rubric, four to five main categories emerged, including content, mode/genre, grammar and mechanics, and project publication.

Immediately following our brainstorming session, students began creating their poetry. Over the next several days, as time would allow, student groups worked together; I traveled from group to group, looking at the writing or researching, trying to address any misconceptions quickly through short, differentiated strategy conferences. Sometimes errors resulted when peers who had edited their work advised them incorrectly. By having the student retrieve their writing folders, I could look at the edits and determine who exactly needed the extra instruction.

As I circulated around the classroom I noticed that the students were working together more closely than before. They politely asked each other questions about the content or the word choices. I was surprised to note that they wanted input throughout the writing process, not just when editing at the end. Wondering about this change, I asked Mayda why she was asking Rachel about what to include in her poem.

"Well, Mrs. Ramsay," she said, "Rachel read my letter and I read hers. She helped me find the Web site to find more interesting information. Since we did this together, I think she can help me become a better writer of poetry."

I was impressed and amazed. In just a short time, through this experience, my students had started viewing one another as valuable learning resources. I was witnessing the formation of their PLNs.

As with the letter-writing activity, I used the basic rubric that the students created for assessment. I scored their poems, leaving comments, and then I met with each student in a short conference to set personal writing goals for the next writing activity (see Box 2.4).

Box 2.4 Student-Created Poetry Rubric

Two versions of our rubric are included here. One, Figure 2.2, is the student version with which they scored one another. The other, Figure 2.3, is the rubric that I created for easy referral to previous goals. My version of the rubric has point values associated with each of the categories.

Reading the students' comments makes me smile. Quite often I find terminology that I've used with them, which shows that they see themselves as teachers trying to assist their peers in improving their writing.

We have a motto in our classroom, "You can always do more, but never less." Several students wanted to create more than one poem. Other students wanted to write poems with partners after they had written their solo versions. Some wanted to include an illustration that they had drawn and scanned or photographs they had taken. They all were able to express themselves in creative ways. (See Figure 2.4 for an example of a letter and the poem created from the information in the letter.)

Through their writing, I could see that their knowledge of habitats, ecosystems, and biomes far exceeded the state-required curriculum, as did their understanding of poetry. I knew what they needed to know to meet the state standards, but the students went beyond this in establishing criteria for this project. They had set higher expectations for themselves because they knew that a real audience was going to read their published work.

FIGURE 2.2

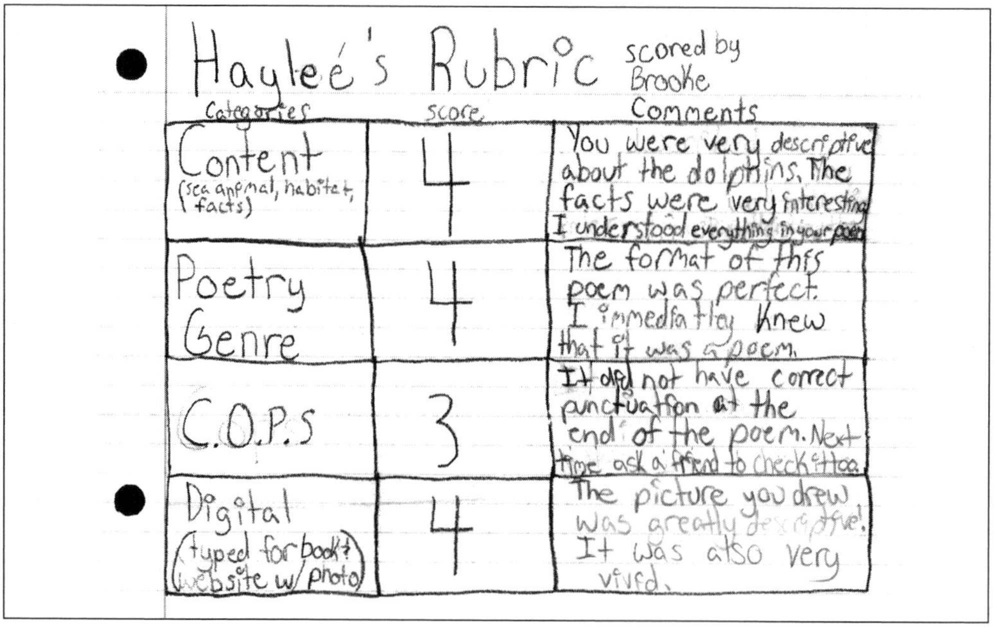

Hayleé's Rubric scored by Brooke

Categories	Score	Comments
Content (sea animal, habitat, facts)	4	You were very descriptive about the dolphins. The facts were very interesting. I understood everything in your poem
Poetry Genre	4	The format of this poem was perfect. I immediatley knew that it was a poem.
C.O.P.S	3	It did not have correct punctuation at the end of the poem. Next time ask a friend to check it too.
Digital (typed for book? website w/ photo)	4	The picture you drew was greatly descriptive! It was also very vivid.

Box 2.4	**Student-Created Poetry Rubric** *(continued)*

Ocean Poetry—September

Student	Content Animal/ Habitat (25 points)	Poetry Genre (25 points)	Editing Using COPS (25 points)	Digital Publishing (25 points)	Teacher's Comments	Student's Personal Goals
Elise	25 points	20 points	20 points	25 points	Great content; watch rhythm of each line poetry; punctuation of poem (90%)	Edit more carefully to be sure word choices make sense; watch capitalization in poems
Juan Carlos	25 points	15 points	15 points	25 points	Confusing wording; difficult to understand; spelling; homophone confusion (80%)	Check spelling; choose words that make sense to a reader
Addy	25 points	15 points	20 points	25 points	What type of poem is this? Think of audience when writing. (85%)	Remember audience; write with characteristics of poetry (genre)
Quinn	20 points	20 points	20 points	15 points	Edit punctuation carefully. Poem typed as paragraph in book, no illustration. (75%)	Punctuate carefully; publishing writing so it's easy for audience to read
Oliver	15 points	25 points	25 points	25 points	Reader needs to know more than just diet; nice use of possessives (90%)	Include content knowledge in writing
Ricky	25 points	10 points	25 points	25 points	Nice use of supporting facts; paragraph written not a poem (85%)	Use characteristics of genre when writing—like we discuss as a class
Elisha	25 points	25 points	20 points	25 points	Great content and descriptive writing; be careful of spelling (90%)	Check spelling; don't rely on Spell Check

FIGURE 2.3

Box 2.4   **Student-Created Poetry Rubric** *(continued)*

Dear Haylee,

We have been reading the *Island of the Dolphins* in class too. We learned some interesting facts about these amazing marine animals. We learned that dolphins eat fish, cephalopods, plankton, and crustaceans. Dolphins can swim up to 5 to12 kilometers per hour. Dolphins have been interacting with humans for as long as we have known about their existence. Dolphins can not go in a deep sleep, only half their body at a time because if they do they would suffocate. Dolphins live up to 40 to 50 years. Most dolphins do not drink the salt water because it is to salty for them to drink! We also know what dolphins do for fun, they are very playful and love to play with whales. All dolphins and whales can produce complex sounds, its for communication or navigation underwater. It's usually clicking, moans, whistles, trills, and squeaks. Dolphins live in all seas except polar seas. Dolphins live in harbors, bays, lagoons and gulfs. Some dolphins like deeper and colder water. Dolphins have a smooth lightweight body so they can move quickly in the water. Dolphins are popular with humans because they are graceful and beautiful creatures. Well, Haylee that's some of the really cool facts that I learned about dolphins. Hope to get a letter from you soon!
      Your friend,
      Brenna

The Dolphin
By: Haylee

She swims in the sea up to 260 miles,
Eating fish of all kind
It could be cod, mackerel, or squid
But not all at one time.

She hits a shark not with sparks but with her gills.
She sees a whale at first sight and wants to play all night.
Then they will swim together until its time to go home.

FIGURE 2.4 Students shared their new knowledge of marine life by writing letters. Here is a poem my student Haylee wrote using the information gained from her e-pal and the artwork that she created to accompany her poem.

Continuing to Go Above and Beyond

I had not realized how much students enjoyed having a rubric while they worked until recently. One day I was sick and absent from school. The day before, we had received our e-pal letters, and one student had printed copies for everyone to read. My intention was that we would spend the next morning sharing our letters and creating a rubric before beginning the next letter. Unfortunately, I was sick the day we were going to share our letters. I asked the substitute teacher to pass out the letters to the students and convey the message that we would discuss them and create a rubric for the next letter when I returned.

However, when I returned the following day, I saw that some students were already writing their letters and referring to a new rubric.

I said, "I like your rubric. Did you come up with it on your own?"

Breayana replied, "Yes and no. I helped, but our team discussed it and came up with it yesterday because we wanted to write. Is that okay?"

"Breayana, you are amazing," I said. "I'm so disappointed that I missed out on your awesome writing and teamwork."

"That's okay, Mrs. Ramsay," she said, reassuring me. "You'll be here next time."

I certainly looked forward to that moment. Each of these experiences gave me confidence that the time and effort that I had invested in creating a more student-centered classroom was worth the huge reward.

A Balancing Act

The e-pals activity was spontaneous and a bit time-consuming initially. We have very stringent guidelines for our class schedules and curriculum pacing guides. Stepping away from these requirements, however briefly, meant that I was out of sync before we began writing the poetry. I had to find a way to balance the mandated lessons with our new project.

I mentioned our dilemma, and the students suggested a few ideas, including skipping PE class (that was a no), taking some of the work to lunch (also a no), or coming in before the start of the regular school day. Although most of those options were not viable, I was pleased that they valued our writing projects so much that they would willingly sacrifice activities they also enjoyed. How often do students volunteer to give up their free time to stay in the classroom and work, write, or create?

As I reviewed our schedule, I found a few slots where we could work poetry activities into our daily routine. Many of my students arrived on buses in the morning, almost an hour before school began. Rather than sitting in the gymnasium or the cafeteria waiting for classes to start, they could come to the classroom and work, if they so desired. During the past few years, almost all of my students have chosen to come early to work. Some arrange for their rides to drop them at school early so they can have extra time to work on their projects.

Students found other ways to complete their writing project during learning center time or small-group instruction time throughout the week. If I was working with a group at the back table and students in other groups had completed their assignments, they could return to their writing project.

Were these times ideal? No. I would have loved to have had an hour or more each day to focus on writing, but that was not possible with all the other guidelines that I was required to follow. Yet despite these constraints, my students still flourished. They recognized that if something is important enough to do, we can find a way to accomplish it.

Chain Reaction

After communicating with my distance-learning collaborating teacher, we decided to expand the project. When her students received the poetry book from my students, my partner asked her students to write fables about each of the animals. The assignment aligned with her state's mandated curriculum. Because her students also wanted to have their work posted online, she let them record their fables as podcasts that could be placed on their class Web site. We did something similar later in the school year (see Chapter 6).

As we read copies of the fables in the e-pals' next correspondences, my students noticed details that had come from their poetry project. The recursive teaching process occurred because of their interest and energy, not because of an artificial assignment. They had the opportunity to see evidence of their work through the writing of other students.

"I wonder what makes these a fable," I said out loud.

After reading and then listening to the podcast versions of the fables, we identified characteristics of the genre. They drew conclusions fairly quickly, much more easily than when I had assigned a fable to read and asked them to respond to a list of questions or facts that I had compiled and disseminated.

I've used this type of learning exchange several times since then. Although the topic may change from year to year—some years it focuses on a certain author, the community, the environment, or inventions—the process remains the same. This point also remains constant: Whenever students have a personal stake in their learning and the permission to follow their passions, they make immediate and profound discoveries that surpass any goals their teachers or policymakers may set.

3

Storytelling for This Generation

Standards and Skills

- Research and inquiry: The American Revolution

- Collaboration

- Critical thinking, problem solving, and decision making

- Narrative, expository, and descriptive writing

- Self-assessment

- Digital citizenship

Technology Tools

- Photo Story (free software)

- Digital videos to build background knowledge

One Thursday morning while making the long trek down the still-quiet hallways toward my classroom, my mind was preoccupied with all the things that I needed to accomplish that day. As I rounded the corner, I saw a small group of students camped out in front of the classroom door. Their heads were bent together in a serious discussion, but they looked up and smiled as I approached.

"We thought you'd never get here," they said, with relief.

I unlocked the classroom door, and they hurried in, taking my laptop bag and carrying what they had been working on while in the hallway. As the rest of the students were sitting in the bus room waiting for classes to start, these students set up the laptop and diligently worked for the next forty-five minutes.

More, Please

Whether working before, during, or after school, my students couldn't get enough of writing lessons supported by an array of digital tools. Because of the way my students were thriving with technology-infused writing projects, I knew that I would have to learn more about free, easy-to-use tools that would slake their amazing thirst for learning. As I watched them writing and creating, the looks in their eyes seemed to say, "More, please."

In searching for quality professional development, I found a webinar series offered by ISTE. (See Chapter 2 for more details about webinars.) Many webinars share projects that integrate technology across grade levels and subjects, so I always extend an invitation to the faculty to join me during the after-school sessions. And then I had a brainstorm: Why not invite students to join me as well? I didn't set firm criteria; I issued an open invitation, and those students who wanted to participate could do so as long as they obtained written permission from their parents and transportation home at the conclusion of the webinar.

The opportunity to interact with adults is always a draw for students in the intermediate and middle grades. I wasn't sure if they would be interested in or able to absorb the content of the webinars, but I hoped they would learn something about professional behavior and expectations. I also knew that in a couple of years they would probably encounter webinars in their academic pursuits, and I wanted them to have the confidence to jump into a learning opportunity in this venue, becoming leaders among their peers.

The first ISTE webinar that I signed up for was on digital storytelling. Six of my students—Ashlyn, Sean, Rachel, Matthew, Elizabeth, and Kynslee—were able to attend this webinar with me and several other faculty members. My initial reason for choosing this webinar was because narrative is one of the writing modes tested on Alabama's standardized assessments. I also hoped that the webinar would offer some additional strategies for teaching storytelling using tools and formats that might appeal to my students. However, I discovered that digital storytelling has a much broader scope than I ever imagined.

The focus of the webinar was on how digital storytelling could enhance learning and how teachers could effectively evaluate students' work products. It was not just a how-to session, which pleased me because it reinforced my goal of using technology to deepen students' understanding of the content standards.

One of the points made in the webinar was that students should be moving away from "about" presentations—those that merely summarize information—and toward higher-level presentations that draw conclusions and make applications with the information they learn. I started thinking about how I could incorporate these suggestions to enhance writing instruction as well as mastery of standards across the content areas.

At the conclusion of the webinar, I escorted the students to their awaiting rides. As usual, I had to fight the urge to lead the conversation as we walked. Having realized the benefit of listening to my students' voices, I knew I would gain a deeper understanding of their point of view if I just waited a little longer before offering my opinions. Sure enough, they did not disappoint me.

"Those digital stories by the second graders were impressive," Matthew said.

Elizabeth agreed: "They are so smart."

"I wish we could have done digital stories in second grade," Kynslee said.

"Yes," Rachel agreed, "but we'll get to do them now. Most other kids won't get to do that either."

"You know," Sean said, "we could make a sample digital story for the class to see, maybe even to teach the other students."

All heads turned toward Sean, and the students' eyes lit up. The conversation quickened, and they were so excited that they talked over one another.

"Mrs. Ramsay could use it in her lessons," Ashlyn said. "Then we could each help the teams make one of their own."

"What would be our subject?" Elizabeth wondered.

"Whatever it is, that lady on the webinar said it was content first," Sean responded.

"Right," Rachel thought out loud. "What if we used it in social studies? I think we'll be studying a war soon. I'll have to look in our textbook to see what comes next."

"But we can't just tell about the war," Matthew reminded the group. "The webinar said we had to relate it to our lives or something."

They were quiet for a minute and then Rachel said, "Let's go home and look at our [textbook] chapter on that and maybe we can brainstorm some ideas. Mrs. Ramsay, would it be okay if we meet you before school to start working? We need to write everything down and plan our story out."

I was elated! These ten- and eleven-year-olds had not only understood the webinar but also were using the information to think like teachers. My mouth said, "Sure, I'd be happy to see you guys in the morning," but my mind was turning cartwheels. What had just happened here? My students had participated in a professional webinar that I had assumed was over their heads, had a quick brainstorming session, planned a digital story to teach their peers, and were working on an idea to help the rest of the students create more digital stories. They understood that the content standards and writing had to come first. Not once did they focus on the technology aspect of the project. They saw the relevance of telling real stories that applied to them today. Now I had to race to keep up with them.

Mining for Gold

I went home and created a time line and checklist to guide my students. I also developed a storyboard graphic organizer to help them plan their writing. I thought that the outlining and sequencing process would be good practice for the narrative prompt on the upcoming standardized writing assessment. I stayed focused on the content and the writing because without that foundation the digital part of the story wouldn't have much substance.

Back at school the next morning, a welcoming party met me again at the classroom door. Before I could share the organizers that I had assembled the night before, the students showed me what they had created. They had talked to each other on the telephone and had collaboratively designed their own time line and storyboard.

We went to the back table where we have small-group instruction, and I asked the students to explain their model. They had chosen to focus on the Revolutionary War, but their background knowledge was extremely limited because we had not studied this yet. I knew they were going to have to read and research more before writing their story. In addition to addressing the curricular goals for writing, literacy, and mechanics, I wanted this digital storytelling project to link them to the past and help them understand the impact that history has on us today. They would have to probe the choices and consequences of the American colonists and the British government during the late eighteenth century.

Of course, at this point I shouldn't have been surprised to discover that the students had already begun some research on their own. They had read the related chapters in our required textbook, talked to family members, and searched for information online.

Our conversation revealed that they were stuck at a superficial level of information—small facts about the war—but their enthusiasm for the subject was inspiring. Whenever they brought up another nugget, I asked, "Why was that important?" They continued to repeat the facts or tell me it was important because it had happened and we had to know it. So I asked, "What happened then that changed who we are today? What would life be like today for us if the colonists hadn't made those choices?"

These types of questions were not new to my students. During my social studies classes, I often guide my students through finding cause-effect relationships, predicting the outcome of events, and making connections between the past and the present. Our social studies discussions lead to some of the most in-depth thinking each day, and we often exceed our mandated time for the class.

I start this kind of questioning from the beginning of the school year, guiding them in finding history's relevance to contemporary issues. They learn that as long as they can justify their answers with good reasoning and examples, their answers will not be judged or graded. In this way, they overcome the fear of being wrong that tends to stifle classroom conversations.

As we were sitting at the table that morning discussing these students' knowledge of the American Revolution, I was surprised that they were struggling to understand the significance of their ancestors' actions. We'd been having these types of discussions for months in class, so I knew that they understood how to reason and draw conclusions. As I started reflecting, I realized that we usually discussed the history story first and then made higher-order connections second. This time the process had been reversed. I had made the mistake of assuming that because they had read the chapter and completed some personal research, they understood both the facts and the context. They had so amazed me with their other thinking regarding this project that I had forgotten that they still needed guidance about how to interpret new information.

Because this group of webinar students asked to continue to come before school and after school a couple of times a week to work on their project, I planned time for us to discuss the American Revolution so they could connect the interesting facts they were compiling into a bigger picture. I pulled some related videos, many from Discovery Education streaming (see Box 3.1), so we could watch and discuss them together. Some of the videos were reenactments; others were interviews with experts. However, the video that appealed most to the students was one that came from American Village, a living history site not far from our school in Montevallo, Alabama. They had produced a video called *Spirit of Liberty*, which reenacted the events leading up to the American Revolution. It tied the relevance of the past to the future while mixing music and narration with the dialogue. Through this resource, the students were able to not only visualize and discuss the importance of the choices made in the production of a digital story but also witness how important it is to connect the past to the present for an audience.

A New Frame of Reference

Once my webinar students had spent several days before and after school building their background knowledge and the big picture of the American Revolution, their conclusions about the relevance of the American Revolution

Box 3.1	**Building Background Knowledge with Digital Videos**

Discovery Education streaming (http://streaming .discoveryeducation.com/) includes an extensive library of student-friendly, nonfiction videos on social studies, science, math, and English that are appropriate across grade levels. Most videos are broken up into smaller segments so that you can select the couple of minutes that may pertain to the lesson that you are teaching at the time. This is not a free service. A site license or membership must be purchased for access to the video library. The Web site states that there are 40,000 video clips that can be directly connected with each state's standards. It also gives teachers access to a high-resolution image library, interactive quiz center, black-line masters and teachers' guides, and a calendar of events that tie video and image content to important dates in history. I encourage you to check it out, perhaps through your school district's IT department. Another nice feature is that the educational videos are not usually blocked by school firewalls and other filtering devices.

Because many of my students have limited background knowledge of world events, Discovery Education streaming has enabled me to easily access content to enhance their understanding of literature, science, math, or social studies. For example, when my students were reading about the Holocaust, I found a video about a boy who had experienced it firsthand; this helped my students connect with the characters in our book. Often during our science conversations,

my students will ask questions about how or why something works. I can usually find a short video clip that explains and demonstrates the answer for them, helping them to connect and understand the content in a much more real way than just a written or verbal explanation.

If you don't have access to Discovery Education streaming, I have found some video clips at sites such as SchoolTube (www .schooltube.com) and TeacherTube (www .teachertube.com). Those sites are not blocked by our school filters, but their video libraries are not as extensive as Discovery Education streaming. Also, the quality can be inconsistent.

One site with high-quality digital videos across content areas is SqoolTube (www.sqooltube .com). The site also includes interactive activities that meet most of the standards my students are expected to master. The site includes clips from Bill Nye the Science Guy, School House Rock, The Magic School Bus, and many others.

Another Web site that provides videos is Next Vista (www.nextvista.org). It has three categories of video collections: Light Bulbs, which introduces topics in the areas of careers, health and fitness, history and culture, literature, math, performing arts, science, technology, visual arts, and writing; Global Views, which promotes understanding of people and their cultures worldwide; and Seeing Service, which highlights the work of people who are working to make this world a better place.

came much easier. I asked, "What was important about the American Revolution that has impacted us today?"

Rachel concluded, "We wouldn't have freedom now."

"What do you mean by freedom?" I asked.

"We would probably still have a king and have no say in government," she responded.

"Yeah," Sean agreed, "we wouldn't be able to have a say in our taxes and laws."

"Tell me how we got that freedom," I continued.

They thought about that for a moment, and then Ashlyn replied, "People like Patrick Henry were willing to speak up for what was right and all of those men were willing to sign the Declaration of Independence even though they knew they were risking their lives."

Elizabeth interrupted, "And the lives of their families."

"Kinda like Rosa Parks in a way," Ashlyn said, connecting with her previous knowledge of the Civil Rights era.

"So how do those people and the freedom that Rachel is talking about apply to us today?" I asked.

"If it weren't for those people risking their lives, we wouldn't be free," Matthew answered.

"Many people died for us too and not just in that war. Freedom isn't free," Rachel concluded.

I gave them a few moments to process this before I asked, "What story do you want to tell about the American Revolution?"

"I think it's important for all of us to think about the price of freedom," Sean said. "Like Rachel said, it's not free. People gave their lives for us to have it. We can't just forget about it." His five teammates agreed with him. They had found their story.

I have been through this process with digital storytelling several times since then. What amazes me is that the students always find a different story to tell. They make unique applications to the present and the future based on what they have learned about the past. It fascinates me to see where their minds take them, often leading them to places that I had not thought about myself.

Finding a Voice

When I initially explored digital storytelling, I thought it would improve our narrative writing lessons and reinforce the required pacing guides, curriculum plans, and standardized test preparation. However, what I discovered was that digital storytelling provided many more opportunities for students to write and create outside of the limited label of narrative writing. My young authors now write across expository, narrative, and descriptive writing modes or genres throughout digital storytelling projects. Students write letters between characters, fictional and nonfictional; create docudramas; conduct interviews; produce television shows; and write comic books. With some guidance, they each select a genre that meets the needs of their story.

Because I let the students choose the various genres in which to write, I decided to revise my initial prewriting planning sheet. Our district provides a prewriting planning sheet for students to use as part of the preparation for the standardized writing assessment. My students have used these prewriting sheets in the Writing Lab class for several years, so they feel comfortable with the tool and use it throughout the writing process. I wanted to create something to guide their thinking and composing while giving them enough freedom to try different formats (see Figure 3.1). Figure 3.2 shows a student's prewriting tool for our digital story project. I have found that this prewriting tool usually will work for any genre of writing. Adding the highlighting direction at the end helps students visualize whether they have focused on their message or just on the "about" aspect of their digital story.

In that first year when my small group of webinar students were embarking on their digital storytelling project, we created a prewriting plan through trial and error. They had determined their topic (the American Revolution) and the message that they wanted to communicate ("Freedom isn't free"). They brainstormed ways to share the message about "the price of freedom" while also teaching their peers about the American Revolution.

FIGURE 3.1
Prewriting Tool

| Topic: _____ |
| Message: What is the lesson that you want people to learn that applies to life today? |
| Introduction: |
| Focus: |
| Conclusion: |
| Highlight the statements or points that you will include that lead to your audience learning your message. |

Digital Story Brooke, Brandon, Jesus, Breayana

Message: What is the lesson that you want people to learn that applies to today? The lesson that we want people to learn that applies to today is that if you are confident and determined like Phillis Wheatley, then you can achieve your most challenging goals.

Introduction: Phillis Wheatley was born in Senegal, Africa in 1753. She had a very difficult life of a slave child of seven. Phillis had an early interest in poetry when she was about twelve years old. The people who owned her soon knew that she was very intelligent and out-going. What they didn't know was that their slave will be a huge benefit to the

Focus: colonists in the war. Phillis Wheatley was very confident in her writing because all though she was a servant and a difficult life, she kept writing and kept sharing her writing with the world. Phillis was also very determined because although people mistreated her and were very prejudice, she kept trying to change the world with writing. When times were tough, she kept a positive outlook and kept moving forward.

Conclusion: Phillis Wheatley benefited the thirteen colonies during the war by encouraging people through her writing. If it wasn't for her we might not have won the war, which would affect the past and even affect today. Her confidence, determination, and positive outlook inspires everyone to make the world a better place.

Highlight the areas that lead to your audience learning your message.

FIGURE 3.2
A group of students used the prewriting tool to create this plan for their digital story.

Then Elizabeth and Rachel came up with the idea of telling the story through letters written between characters. Kynslee and Matthew agreed and suggested that the letters be written by imaginary cousins who lived in key places during the American Revolution, such as Philadelphia and Boston. The students created a time line of important events and dates to ensure that they incorporated accurate details from the period. They divided into pairs, each assuming a name of one of the two imaginary cousins, and decided what should be included in their letters to teach and enlighten. Then each pair took turns verbally composing a letter and sharing it with others before they wrote.

We spent time conferencing each day before school so I could check their writing and focus. Now that they had a stronger understanding of the historical period, a time line of events, and an objective, they gradually needed less and less input from me.

At this point, we did not have a rubric or any type of assessment in place for their writing because they had volunteered to work on this project beyond their regular school work. They did edit each other's work for historical accuracy, organization, grammar, and mechanics, using a method similar to the one they had learned while writing their e-pal letters.

Going Digital

Because digital storytelling was new for me and I didn't have the money to buy software, I found a free tool from Microsoft called Photo Story. Since then, I've discovered that there are many options for creating digital stories, including free open source software, such as Gimp (www.gimp.com), and a wide range of tools for integrating music, transition, and effects. For more information on creating digital stories, see Dr. Helen C. Barrett's (2009) handouts and tutorials at http://electronicportfolios.com/digistory/howto.html. Another helpful site is "The Educational Uses of Digital Storytelling" from the University of Houston (2010) (http://digitalstorytelling.coe.uh.edu/). I chose Photo Story because it was easy to use on our Windows-based laptop. Many teachers have told me that they use Apple's iMovie, but currently we are an all-PC district.

Photo Story creates video using still pictures. After downloading the free software (www.microsoft.com/downloads/en/default.aspx), you can set up a slideshow/video of your digital pictures, adding narration and music. Photo Story has some nice features, such as pan and zoom effects, picture rotation, photo editing, and cropping tools. It also has a built-in feature to allow you to create your own music. Photo Story also lets you share the final project in various ways: through playback on your computer, in an e-mail message, or through playback on a pocket PC or smart phone with Windows Media Player.

While watching the Discovery Education streaming videos, I had drawn the students' attention to the filmmaker's use of music to enhance the feeling of the films. They were surprised to discover that music can help tell a story. That gave them a frame of reference when it came time to add music to their own digital stories.

After they uploaded photos and images to Photo Story and placed them in the correct order to enhance their writing, they used a small microphone to record their voices into Photo Story to narrate the story. The students saved everything into a project file within Photo Story. The last step was to convert the project file into a movie file. With Photo Story, all you have to do is click a button, and voila!

When these webinar students shared their digital stories with their classmates, their peers were very focused and engaged. The webinar students led a discussion about the price of freedom and applied the topic to current events, such as the U.S. military operations in the Middle East. When the presenters suggested that their classmates create their own digital stories focusing on a patriot from the American Revolution whose choices impacted us today, the enthusiasm and excitement were palpable.

Developing the Rubric

Each of the teams collaborated with one of the digital storytelling experts from that initial group of webinar students. The teams formed the categories for a rubric to evaluate the digital storytelling. This rubric differed from previous ones in that it was designed to assess teams, not individuals. It would have to evaluate teamwork and collaboration in addition to writing and technology skills.

Why work in teams? Because of strict time constraints and pacing guides in our school districts, as well as a limited number of computers, I had to compromise. I considered the benefits of letting students fulfill different roles within their teams, experience writing in a new genre, and gain experience with a new technology tool.

Although my students had created other rubrics, I still felt uneasy about their ability to identify all of the important elements in creating a digital story. I was tempted to use one of the rubrics available online but decided to see what the students could come up with on their own. They didn't disappoint me.

Although their rubric was simpler than many online versions, it met the basic criteria of focusing on the written story and making connections and applications to their lives today. There wasn't a lot of debate about which categories to include in this rubric, unlike our experience with previous rubrics. I think one of the differences was that the students had already seen a specific example—that of the webinar students. They could visualize their destination. As we discussed the project, the experts shared their insights about what they had learned about the focus of their digital story: the application of the history content to the present day. They not only modeled the writing and production of their message for the whole class, but they also had experience to draw on as they guided within their small groups (see Box 3.2).

Box 3.2   My Students' Digital Storytelling Rubric

In Figure 3.3 you will see the rubric that the students used with one another and, in Figure 3.4, a version of the rubric that I've used. Both are very similar to the rubrics shown in previous chapters. The major difference is that, for the digital storytelling project, I score teams instead of individuals. I still conference with each team, and in the conference we discuss their team's strengths and weaknesses. I've found that students often already know their skills before we begin the conference. Many times they begin the conference explaining what they should or should not have done in their digital story. Some teams have even requested to go back and make some adjustments before we publish their work on the class Web site and/or share the work with other classes.

As with the other rubrics, this one varies from year to year depending on the students and what

they feel is important to include in their publications. The rubric shown in Figures 3.3 and 3.4 includes the categories of content and message—the factual information that students use to justify their main application of the past to today. It also includes grammar and mechanics and the digital publication, all of which should support the overall lesson that each story is teaching the audience.

The student rubric (Figure 3.3) does not include teamwork as a category, because they do not score other teams on their teamwork—just on their digital story. They only assess their own team members' collaboration skills.

Although this rubric is much simpler than many published rubrics, I have found that student-created rubrics really do work in spurring high-quality, thoughtful composing and creating.

FIGURE 3.3
A Student's Digital Story Rubric

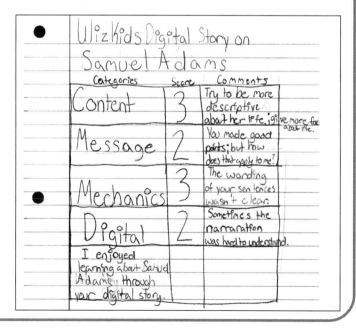

| Box 3.2 | **My Students' Digital Storytelling Rubric** *(continued)* |

Team Name	Content (20 points)	Message (20 points)	Mechanics (20 points)	Digital (20 points)	Teamwork (20 points)	Goals
Wildcats	15 points	20 points	20 points	20 points	20 points	Check accuracy of ALL facts; great message relevant to today; beautiful production supporting message (95%)
Mathletes	20 points	20 points	20 points	10 points	20 points	Your facts support your message; great message; the music overwhelms the narration; nice teamwork throughout project (90%)
Word Wizards	10 points	15 points	20 points	20 points	15 points	Mostly opinion; only one fact; nice application to today; could have been stronger with more facts supporting; great production supporting your writing; good job of working out beginning teamwork disagreements (80%)
Team Unstoppable	20 points	15 points	15 points	20 points	20 points	Great content supporting your message; one point unclear on application of the message; great job supporting your focus with your production (90%)
Tiger Tide	15 points	10 points	15 points	10 points	20 points	More information needed to support your message; good qualities shared about Patriot, but how does it apply to today? Check your subject-verb agreement; great teamwork (70%)
Superstars	20 points	15 points	10 points	20 points	20 points	Be sure that all of your points/facts support the overall message of your story; watch the use of subject-verb agreement; nice teamwork (85%)

FIGURE 3.4 My Class Digital Story Rubric

Meanwhile . . . A Digital Detour

While my young authors were in the process of researching their digital stories based on the Revolutionary War, the class read "The Midnight Ride of Paul Revere" by Henry Wadsworth Longfellow. The language in this elegant but lengthy poem can be difficult to understand, so after we read each couplet I would do a think-aloud to help students interpret the meaning by drawing on their growing knowledge of the time period. We were about halfway through the choral reading when one of my students raised his hand.

"Mrs. Ramsay," he said, "this is still kinda hard to get. But I was thinking that if we turned it into a digital story we might be able to understand it better."

Great idea! Wish I had thought of that. By breaking up the poem and finding an image or creating an illustration to expand on the meaning, we could let all students deepen their reading comprehension and vocabulary skills while dipping their toes into digital technology. I knew the Midnight Ride digital story project wouldn't take much time to complete, because I already had six Photo Story experts and Henry Wadsworth Longfellow had already written the poem. (I was also delighted that my students were intuitively addressing ISTE's [2007] NETS for Students, using Standard 4: Critical Thinking, Problem Solving, and Decision Making.)

The students who had created the first digital stories set up the laptop computer with Photo Story on it in a corner of the classroom. After we assigned different sections of the poem, the students found related images or created illustrations, which they uploaded to a new project file in Photo Story (see Box 3.3 for information about guiding students in their search for copyright-free materials). The digital story experts took turns working with their peers to record the reading of each section of the poem. This was all done during free moments throughout the day while students were continuing with their regular routines. Of course, we had many announcements of "quiet on the set" when they were recording, but the students were generally respectful of one another because they knew that each of them would get a turn to contribute to the production. If I heard a student who was having difficulty explaining or reading, I would pull him or her aside for a one-on-one tutorial. If there was a difference of opinion, I was there to settle the dispute as needed. Later I realized that this process of turning a classic piece of literature into a digital story had enhanced my students' learning far more than I had expected. See Chapter 8 for a complete explanation of how the students were inspired to produce a related video during the last week of the school year.

| Box 3.3 | **Publishing and Copyrights** |

Today students are regularly creating and publishing work for the global community. The issue of fair use and copyright licensing is a very real concern, and students need to know what is appropriate (see ISTE [2007] NETS for Students, 5, Digital Citizenship). I've found that, typically, students don't fully understand the importance of using others' work only with permission, including photos and music easily accessible on the Internet. Once we have a discussion about what it means to "borrow" the work of others, we look at ways for them to locate materials that they can freely use to enhance their writing.

Creative Commons is a nonprofit organization that seeks to increase collaboration through a variety of different licensing conditions, such as attribution, no derivative works, noncommercial, and share alike. You can find comprehensive information about Creative Commons at http://creativecommons.org/.

In my class, we look at the differences among the categories (the types of permissions or rights for publication), and I model a search process. For example, with the Paul Revere project, we search for images and discuss the different licensing that would apply. Many photo Web sites, such as Flickr, have photos categorized by types of Creative Commons licensing agreements, making a search much easier for students. One thing that I stress is that although they may have the permission to incorporate another person's photos, artwork, or music, they still must cite the creator/author of the work used.

When searching for digital support for their writing, my students usually prefer to Google "Creative Commons music" or "Creative Commons photos" instead of visiting a certain Web site. I think they like the hunt that is unique to their project. When my students find work that they want to use for a project, they contact the owner and explain the educational purpose of the project at hand, and the owner will usually extend permission.

Coming Full Circle

In class, we spent two to three days a week studying and discussing the Revolutionary War content during our social studies period, and on the other days during that period, we worked on the patriot digital stories. Having seen the digital story expert students come to work before school, many of the learning teams also wanted to show up early. I used the checklist that the first group of students created, adding a few items, to keep the digital storytelling process on track (see Figure 3.5). The photos or illustrations for a digital story can be created by hand and scanned. They can also be created using drawing tools on the computer, or students can use copyright-free images. The music can be created using Photo Story or found on copyright-free music sites. Although we designed the checklist for Photo Story, you can adapt it for other software programs.

FIGURE 3.5
Digital
Storytelling
Checklist

Digital Storytelling Checklist

_____   Brainstorm ideas

_____   Develop topic

_____   Identify message (the lesson that applies to today
that you want the audience to learn)

_____   Prewrite

_____   Write first draft

_____   Edit

_____   Write final draft

_____   Segment the writing into a storyboard

_____   Create illustrations or add photos

_____   Insert photos in Photo Story

_____   Practice oral reading fluency

_____   Record voice into digital story

_____   Create/add music to enhance your message

_____   Check for any mistakes

_____   Publish as a video file

Managing this collaborative storytelling project was challenging at times. One difficulty was finding an equitable way to evaluate and score the individual contributions the students made to the team project. I created a chart listing the different levels of engagement within the team (see Figure 3.6). I shared this with the students and we discussed how we would use it.

Because I worked with each team at least once on the days they were writing and creating their stories, I thought I had a good basis for knowing how to score each team member's contributions. However, the students had con-

Category	4	3	2	1
Collaboration	Regularly offers productive ideas to the team; fulfills team role; works hard	Usually offers productive ideas to the team; tries hard to fulfill team role	Sometimes offers productive ideas to the team; sometimes fulfills team role; only does what is required	Rarely offers productive ideas to the team; rarely fulfills team role or participates
Cooperation	Mostly listens, shares, and supports team's work and ideas; encourages teamwork	Usually listens, shares, and supports team's work and ideas; does not cause problems for the team	Often listens, shares, and supports team's work and ideas; sometimes is uncooperative	Rarely listens, shares, and supports team's work and ideas; often is uncooperative
Engagement	Always stays engaged in what needs to be done	Usually stays engaged in what needs to be done	Often, with reminders, stays engaged in what needs to be done	Rarely stays engaged in what needs to be done
Critical Thinking	Always looks for ways to solve problems or meet challenges	Usually looks for ways to solve problems or meet challenges	Sometimes looks for ways to solve problems or meet challenges, but tries others' ideas	Rarely looks for ways to solve problems or meet challenges; not willing to try others' ideas
Scheduling	Regularly completes work in a timely manner	Usually completes work in a timely manner	Sometimes completes work in a timely manner, with reminders from team members	Rarely completes work in a timely manner, even with reminders from team members

FIGURE 3.6
Teamwork/
Participation
Chart

cerns that some of their peers would not uphold their part of the job when I was not looking. So we decided that each team member would rate one another in addition to my rating.

One student asked, "But what if they are mad at you and just give you a low score to be mean?"

She made a good point. I asked, "What do you think we could do to prevent this from happening?"

"We could give specific examples of why we give someone a score, like when we give you answers in class," one student suggested.

"But what if two people gang up on someone?" the first student said, worried.

"Then maybe Mrs. Ramsay could talk to them and discover if it's a real problem or not. Like when we have problems anyway," the second student answered.

"So what you're saying is that each team member scores the other members and makes specific comments explaining the score, and then we combine that score with my score for a grade for that week on teamwork. If there are any disputes, we'll discuss those together," I reiterated.

The students agreed that the suggested process would be a fair way to assess teamwork. They seemed really invested in the idea of having a say in the scoring of their team projects. This was something that I had not thought about before—the idea of letting them assess one another with guidelines. I could follow their logic: They created the story project. They created the rubric. So why wouldn't they score the work as well?

I had always done all of the scoring. After all, it affected their grades for the course. But were the students looking to assess one another for a grade? No. Grades for the grade book were not mentioned. Project completion and teamwork were the concerns. This shift from learning for grades to learning for enjoyment had happened when they started writing their e-pal letters. They were writing to an authentic audience, striving to meet their personal writing goals.

Without question, the students were creating these digital stories not only for one another but also to post for their writing friends across the country who were also studying American history. They also suggested that we share these stories with the other fifth-grade classes at our school. Later, we discovered that the third-grade classes were reading a story that had a setting of the American Revolution, so we shared our stories with them as well.

Now that the students had an audience for their creations and wanted to become accountable to each other through their rubric, I decided to let them score one another's digital stories while I simultaneously scored the projects using their rubric. My thought was that if the students did not score each other equitably, I could just use my scoring as the final grade for the project.

Our classroom became a digital story production whirlwind. Any time students completed their other course work they would work on their digital stories. In this whirlwind, I took opportunities to refocus students and get them to reach a deeper understanding as I circulated among working groups. One group focused on John Adams. When I met with the team members I asked,

"What was special about John Adams?" They responded with a list of his accomplishments. I asked, "Why are those accomplishments important?" They listed the accomplishments again. "But why are those things important for us to know?" Blank stares. I gave them time to think, then asked, "How would our lives today be different if John Adams and other men and women like him didn't do those things you listed?" Confused looks. More time to get the brains in gear. "What do you think our country would be like today if those people had not made the choices that they did?"

Kevin said, "You mean like we would have a king still telling us what to do?"

"Good," I said. "What else would be different?"

The other group members jumped in, making a list of civil rights that might not be possible without the sacrifices made by Americans during the Revolutionary period. The list included some wonderful fifth-grade twists, including singing "The Star-Spangled Banner," having a say in what our taxes pay for, and being able "to go home and watch the Vikings play football this weekend because we would have to do what the king said and he probably wouldn't like football."

The students' rapid conversation and contributions continued. These were their answers, not mine. They owned that project because of their personal stake in the interpretation.

Just as with the original webinar group, the focus was on writing the meaningful story and emphasizing relevant information first, and only then enhancing their learning by sharing it in a digital format. Because each team had an "expert" member, they had someone who could walk them through any technical difficulties that might arise.

One day, as I was traveling from team to team, I overheard a conversation between Elizabeth and her team. She said, "I think we need to change this picture on this slide to another one. Look, this one is dark and foggy. It looks spooky, making you feel a bit scared, which is probably what they felt risking their lives for freedom."

"I wouldn't want to go in that picture," Tony said. "Someone might jump out and get you."

"Right," Elizabeth continued. "It would have been scary to do what the Sons of Liberty did. This picture is perfect."

Elizabeth, the expert in her group, guided her teammates in making choices that would support their story. Without her leadership, the feeling of their story may not have been as powerful to the audience. Having experts on each team helped to alleviate many of the hands in the air for answers to small items and questions. When students have a question, they often shut down the

Student Reflection

Kevin Valladares, fifth-grade student

In digital stories, while processing, you have to think what you're going to write about. That means that digital stories start off as content and then evolve into wonderful sounds in your ears by using Photo Story 3. Before I get any further into using digital stories, I'm going to announce how we created and started our digital story. We first were talking about important people writing and double checking the Declaration of Independence. We chose to write about John Adams. We had a hard time thinking about what to do. So we went and looked at a sheet of paper that had different kinds of writing, and we saw comics. My friend Steven and I were good at comics, so our group decided to do a comic digital story. Then we had to think about how we were going to do it. Our teacher and group decided to do it about how if John Adams never lived. So now we have our own John Adams digital story. I loved doing this instead of on a poster board because I think you learn so much more using technology than our parents did in like the 1930s. This is the 21st Century and we have technology now to help us learn better.

working process and wait. Waiting leads to boredom and lack of focus, which often leads to off-task, disruptive behavior. For a teacher, trying to prevent this cascade can be extremely frustrating because you can only be at one place at a time. I've heard many teachers complain that this is why they don't implement more technology projects to support their curriculum. My solution is to have experts in the classroom who can answer and solve minor problems or questions. Then I can really focus on discussing the writing and the content and guiding the teams in their choices throughout the process.

After students completed the digital stories, we arranged to have a screening day to present and evaluate all the projects before we published them on our Web site and invited friends, family, and other classes to view them.

Each student scored each of the digital stories, including their own, using the student-created rubric. Each team then averaged the scores given to each story by the members of that team and compiled the comments to turn into me. They gave their individual score sheets to the team whose story they had just scored. I took the six student-scored rubrics (one per team) and averaged them. That score represented 50 percent of the grade, and my score would represent the other 50 percent, unless I found a major discrepancy. Each individual turned in participation scores for his or her team members.

I discovered that the students' assessments of one another were usually aligned with my reviews. The same consistency has shown up every time I have used this type of assessment. The idea to require comments to justify scoring choices seems to weed out most of the petty or vindictive marks. Giving students a voice beyond just creating a rubric really brought this project full circle. My students were empowered to control not only the process but also the final outcome.

(For examples of the digital stories mentioned in this chapter, see www .stenhouse.com/skiplunch.)

CHAPTER

4

One Size Does Not Fit All

Standards and Skills
- Oral reading fluency
- Expository writing
- Poetry composition
- Collaboration

Technology Tools
- Jing (software)
- VoiceThread (http://voicethread.com)

In 2006, when I began pursuing certification in the Middle Childhood Generalist category from the National Board for Professional Teaching Standards, I gained a much deeper understanding of the critical importance of differentiated instruction, an educational practice that I had previously thought of as a buzzword or another trend of the moment. The National Board Certification process requires teachers to demonstrate and provide evidence of reaching all learners, not just those who are easiest to teach. As the educator and author Rick Wormeli writes, "The two simple charges of differentiation are: (1) do whatever it takes to maximize students' learning instead of relying on a one-size-fits-all, whole-class method of instruction and (2) prepare students to handle anything in their current and future lives that is not differentiated, i.e., to become their own learning advocates" (2007, 9).

Although I thought I had strong whole-group lessons, going through the National Board Certification process required me to focus on my small-group instructional strategies and reflect on their effectiveness. What I discovered was that some of my students were quietly slipping through the cracks in each content area.

In addition to reading books and articles about good differentiation practices, I consulted colleagues who always seemed to have individual students in mind instead of just the class as a whole. From Vicki I learned that by spending most of the day working with small groups, teachers could know students better and respond to their needs immediately. Tina also shared helpful tips for managing a classroom with such a focus. One of the changes I made based on their suggestions was to keep an ongoing record of each student's writing strengths, weaknesses, and goals (see Chapter 1). This resource not only shows me what to nurture or draw out in my students but also gives the students data to observe their own progress and set their own goals. While assessing each student at the completion of a writing project, I take notes about specific skill gaps they may have. Then I group students with similar skill gaps and design a lesson to target their needs.

After the positive experiences of using technology to enrich our e-pal exchanges and the digital storytelling project, I thought I might search for some new tools and strategies to help students who were struggling with oral language. Although verbal proficiency might seem like an odd topic to address in a book about writing instruction, I think you'll see how these two strands of communication unite beautifully through technology-assisted learning.

Speak Up

Our school district requires teachers to regularly assess students' oral reading fluency (ORF) to find ways to improve reading comprehension and writing. In addition to the data I collect from the mandated assessments, I use formative assessments, such as observing how students ask and answer questions, interact with peers, and perform during small-group oral reading sessions. In our heterogeneous learning teams, I purposefully include a job that requires someone to speak or present publicly. This job (along with the other positions) rotates each week so that I can assess students' growth in oral communication over time.

For instance, one of my students has an identified learning disability in reading. He struggles to read unfamiliar passages out loud, but he scores very well on formal reading assessments when he can read silently and take time to decode words. He also comprehends well when he listens to someone read aloud, and he speaks very well in peer interactions and class discussions. His formal ORF scores are far below grade-level standards, but because I use those other formative assessments, I get a much clearer view of his needs and abilities.

In addition to the formal and informal data that I gather about students' language proficiency, throughout our digital storytelling project I observed that several students had a difficult time with the oral reading and recording portions. My classes usually include English language learner (ELL) students, struggling readers (those performing below grade level), and some with exceptional needs. Generally, these students also lack self-esteem because by fifth grade they have been told numerous times that they are not meeting the mandated ORF standards. I was determined to help them become successful, and technology gave me a wonderful new tool to sharpen their learning.

Jing, Jing

I searched online for resources that would give my students an authentic way to communicate orally. After some time, I found an archived webinar that demonstrated a free Web 2.0 tool called Jing (see Box 4.1), which adds visual elements to your online conversations. Jing is software that enables you to capture anything you create or see on your computer screen and share it with others as an image or as part of a slideshow or movie. You can narrate the steps of an application on the computer and create a tutorial that includes audio and visual components. You also can add arrows to point to a section on the screen, create textboxes to highlight or summarize information, and position your computer mouse or cursor to show where to click for an Internet link.

After using Jing at home, I demonstrated the software to a group of students the next day at school. Because these students struggled with oral language, I didn't want to burden them with too many steps at once. I asked them to create a short video tutorial explaining how to use *Photo Story*, the software we had adopted for our digital stories. This assignment would target not only their oral fluency but also their writing, communicating, and collaborating skills. They also would be contributing to our distance learning project with the students in another state.

Watching these students investigate Jing, I noticed that they were very enthusiastic about experimenting with the software and being the first in the class to try it. However, when they discovered that they would have to give oral directions, they paled. "Oh, we record our voice?" one student lamented. "It's going to take me a million times to get it right." I told her that there wasn't any

Box 4.1   **Using Jing**

A free download of Jing for Windows or Macintosh can be found at www.techsmith.com/jing/. The free version lets you record up to five minutes of onscreen action. Jing provides video tutorials that explain how to create your own projects. After you have finished the project, you can upload it to Screencast.com or Flickr. The videos are available immediately, and you can even add a Jing to a tweet on Twitter. Jing Pro, the paid version of the software, lets you use webcam video, edit your videos, create longer segments, and upload your creations to YouTube, among other things.

Here are a few ideas for using Jing in the classroom:

- Demonstrate school procedures or projects to students' families.

- Share photos or video of classroom activities.
- Explain a difficult concept that students may want to review several times throughout a unit.
- Teach other teachers and students how to use a new Web tool.
- Record comments or evaluations for students and their parents.
- Send comments and demonstrations to students who are homebound or absent for long periods of time.
- Let students create a project explaining what they learned from a unit of study and how it applies to their lives.

A word of caution: Make sure that the sites involved in using Jing are not blocked by your school district's security filters.

rush to get it done quickly; she could spend as much time as she needed to feel comfortable with her recording. I also told the students that they could record the segments while the others were out of the classroom if that would make them feel more secure. The worry lines vanished and they soon devised a plan.

A New Platform and Purpose

The students in the Jing group realized that they would first have to write the directions for using Photo Story and then read and record the steps. I encouraged them to start talking and listening to one another, create a work plan, write a script, and then practice reading the script out loud.

Although these students often became frustrated more quickly than others, they never lost momentum with this project. As one of them said, "Everyone else is depending on us; we have to get this right, guys." They focused on communicating to the audience, not on themselves.

Sidestepping Obstacles

After several revisions, the students completed their Jing tutorial and were ready to upload it to Screencast.com. I had practiced using the software at home and thought it would be a simple process that I could walk these students through at school. However, once we went to the Screencast.com Web site, we found that it was blocked by our district server. Unfortunately, this was not a new discovery for us; we had tried several different technology tools throughout the year and found that our productions were often blocked by security filters. The students would wryly say, "I guess they don't want us to learn today. Don't they know what awesome things we could do?"

But this time I was mentally screaming, "Not again!" These students had overcome so many obstacles to reach this level. They needed to share their success with others. I followed the usual protocol of submitting an e-mail request to the district technology department, asking for unrestricted access to the Web site. When I didn't hear back, I sent another request. And again. Sometimes, with the assistance of an administrator or our school media specialist, we can get a site unblocked, but the access often proves temporary. After a few hours, the site is blocked again.

I asked the students if they had any ideas. They suggested that I upload the Jing tutorial from my home. I went online and asked my PLN for other solutions. Several colleagues urged me to go around the district's server or break through the filters. I did not feel comfortable with those suggestions. I didn't want to teach my students that it was okay to circumvent the system, no matter how justified our actions may be.

In the end, I did upload the Jing tutorial from home, but that meant that my students couldn't watch it from school. Many of my students do not have computer access at home and they don't have transportation to the public library unless they live close enough to walk, so they never got to see the final project.

The good news is that students at our partner school and some in our own classroom were able to view the Jing project. The creators were so excited. Many of their peers commented on how glad they were to have the tutorial to watch at home because they were trying to create digital stories and had gotten stuck on a step. My formerly struggling readers got a big boost of confidence and improved their ORF test scores.

Despite the setbacks with Jing, all of my students wanted to use it to demonstrate and teach the other technology tools that we had adopted in our classroom. They offered compelling arguments, but I wondered if we might find other software that would enable me to provide differentiated instruction as well as sail through the district's server channels.

VoiceThread

An answer came from Mary O'Brien, a third-grade teacher from Maine who is a member of my PLN. Mary sent me an invitation to view a VoiceThread

---

Box 4.2   Using VoiceThread

VoiceThread is a truly collaborative tool. To begin using it, you visit http://voicethread.com/ and register. There is nothing to download; all the work is done online. I chose to register for the free educator's account. Other options require a fee, but the free account gave me all the features that I needed.

Once I registered, I created an identity for each student. I gave them unique usernames by adding our school's initials to the beginning of their first names. You can also upload a photo of each student if you like. Easy tutorials that pop up when you register for VoiceThread will show you what to do.

VoiceThread lets you create a slideshow of images and text, including photographs, artwork, videos, documents, and classroom presentations. After uploading the project, participants can have a conversation about the VoiceThread project through voice, text, or doodling (similar to what television sportscasters do when they analyze a football formation). All of these options are found on the Comment button. The person commenting can always delete and rerecord or retype their remarks, and you can access the discussion from anywhere at any time so that time zones are not a hindrance to the collaborative conversations. Another useful feature is the Zoom-In option, which lets users enlarge a document or image that has been uploaded to the project.

Once you create a VoiceThread, you can invite people to view it or let them edit it. You also have the ability to set the levels of privacy. We invited other classes to edit our VoiceThread projects, but made them available to the general public for viewing only. That way anyone could see it, but only the students involved in our collaborative online journal could make additions.

My students love this tool because they are able to have conversations about the images, hear different points of view, and learn from one another regardless of age or geographic location.

---

project that her students had created about their school. She walked me through the steps of showing my students how to record their voices or make written comments on each of the photographs that her students had included in their VoiceThread project (see Box 4.2).

Love the Earth Poetry

As I watched my students make clever and humorous observations as they viewed Mary O'Brien's students' school handbook project in VoiceThread, I realized that this tool could help me tailor instruction to more than one group at a time. This insight led to the creation of a distance learning collaborative project that has since grown to include more than 200 second through sixth graders in five states. Like most of our technology-assisted projects, this one started by pursuing an interest, searching for ways to tie it to the curriculum, building on what we already knew, and exploring new options for learning. In this case, my students were using Moodle (see Chapter 1) to discuss the next theme for the online journal they planned to publish with their e-pals. Through discussion they decided to focus on "going green," an exploration of environmental stewardship.

With the theme of "going green" in mind, one of the students suggested that we create environmental poetry. (This was a different group of students during a different school year than the ones who had written the sea life poetry; see Chapter 2.) I saw this as an opportunity to give students more time to practice a new technology tool (VoiceThread), write free-verse poetry using figurative language, reach out to a wider audience, and pursue their interest in individual topics within the framework of environmental studies. At the same time, I could attend to the needs of different learners.

My colleague Staci Moore Hawkins, our school's writing specialist who is always interested in trying new things to improve the students' writing schoolwide, offered to help us with this project. She conducted some of the individual writing conferences with students so I would have more time to work with small groups on other areas. Staci also attended a workshop about using VoiceThread and practiced at home so she could teach the students how to upload their poetry and illustrations as well as record their voices. She often gave up her planning periods to work with my students. With her assistance and insights, we were able to complete the environmental poetry project in a week. More important, my students and I loved having another person in the school building with whom to share our enthusiasm for technology-supported writing.

After uploading their poetry and illustrations, my students took turns recording and adding typed comments to the work of their classmates (Figure 4.1). Finally, we sent invitations to our collaborators in other states to add to

FIGURE 4.1
Two students
work on
recording their
comments for
our class
VoiceThread
project.

our VoiceThread project and then made it available for public viewing. We published a link to the final project in our online journal. (The rubrics we used to score the poems in the project are described in Box 4.3.) Because VoiceThread conversations are archived, I have been able to access this project in subsequent years so new students can use it in class discussions or for differentiated learning, and they can add to the conversation as well.

Box 4.3 Rubric for Writing Love the Earth Poetry Using VoiceThread

As with other projects, we used two rubrics. The first, shown in Figure 4.2, indicates how the students scored one another, and the second, shown in Figure 4.3, shows the records I used to help them set their own writing goals. You will notice that the rubrics are scored like those described in previous chapters and that my students tend to use similar categories. Depending on the project, they usually include the topic, the form of writing, and the characteristics of the genre or mode. They also give points for editing, grammar, and the quality of the digital components. Other rubrics that you find or create as a teacher will probably be much more in-depth and specific. However, this is a rubric to guide the students in accomplishing their goals. Their rubrics address the standards they must meet, and if they leave off something important I redirect them.

Notice that the focus is always on the subject content and the writing, not on the technology tool. Usually the tools are mentioned in relation to how they enhance the students' messages. This is no different from how teachers have historically assessed students' abilities to use outside resources or research. For example, years ago when we asked students to refer to encyclopedias for research papers, we did not focus on the student's ability to use an encyclopedia but on the writing process and final result. Technology tools support real learning and thinking, but the tools themselves come and go. Students are the constant in a classroom, and our job is to give them the skills to be productive global citizens both for today and tomorrow.

FIGURE 4.2

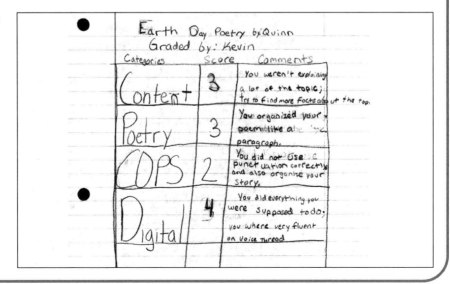

| Box 4.3 | **Rubric for Writing Love the Earth Poetry Using VoiceThread** *(continued)* |

Love the Earth Poetry—VoiceThread

Student	Content (25 points)	Poetry (25 points)	Editing Using COPS (25 points)	Digital (25 points)	Teacher's Comments	Student's Personal Goals
Lene	25 points	25 points	20 points	25 points	Nice job teaching about an environmental issue; nice use of rhyme; watch poetry punctuation (95%)	Remember to punctuate poetry; watch for end marks at end of thoughts
Jairo	10 points	25 points	10 points	25 points	What was your focus/issue? Nice use of alliteration; check your spelling; nice expression on your reading (70%)	Double- and triple-check my spelling; pay attention to the prompt
Carmen	25 points	15 points	25 points	20 points	Good job sharing your concerns; be careful to organize your thoughts; sentence end punctuation. Focus on your articulation. (85%)	Watch organization—have other people read writing to make sure that it makes sense to the audience
Jillian	20 points	20 points	15 points	25 points	Be sure to have information that supports your message; edit carefully to catch spelling and capitalization errors (80%)	Justify my points clearly to audience; take time to edit for careless errors
Felix	25 points	20 points	25 points	25 points	Nice job supporting the issue and creating rhyming couplets; descriptive language could help the audience to visualize better (95%)	Use descriptive language (figurative language and adjectives) to help audience "see" my writing
Gaige	20 points	20 points	25 points	25 points	Nice choice of issue, but what do you want the audience to do about it? Watch homophones. (90%)	Watch my word choice with homophones; follow through the entire prompt
Roberta	25 points	25 points	15 points	20 points	Fun poem to hear; watch your subject-verb agreement; be careful about pacing in oral reading (85%)	Use correct subject-verb agreement every time I write

FIGURE 4.3

One Project, Multiple Ways to Learn

While we were working on the environmental poetry project, I targeted three groups for special attention. One group of students was struggling with articulation when recording for VoiceThread. Another group needed additional lessons on writing with the correct subject-verb agreement. Yet another group of students needed more practice using descriptive language to help the audience to see, hear, or feel the subject of their compositions.

The Art of Articulation

The group targeted in this section included two special-needs students who struggled with oral fluency, particularly articulation. They both received special education services identified in their individualized education plans (IEPs), but it was still difficult to understand them, especially in voice recordings. The speech and language pathologist, Gayle Craft, and I decided to emphasize the importance of being understood by an audience of peers to motivate these students to improve their speaking skills. Gayle graciously offered to work with these two students on their fluency and articulation in addition to the time I would spend with them in small-group sessions. We asked them to record their poems and provide at least one verbal comment on another student's poem.

As the students were beginning to record the audio segments, one of the special-needs students approached me and asked, "Mrs. Ramsay, would it be okay if I practice with Brooke?" His question showed me that he obviously understood the importance of practicing, the strength of working with others, and his responsibility to make improvements himself. That was huge progress for this student. With a lot of work and practice, he was able to reach his goal of publishing and recording his voice in our VoiceThread project.

The other special-needs student had different challenges. He quickly learned his poem by working with me, the speech pathologist, and peers. However, when it came time for him to record his verbal comments, he would ramble on and on, and the listener couldn't understand what he was saying. He wasn't transferring his knowledge from the poem to his informal conversation. When I asked him to listen to his poem and then to his verbal comments and contrast the two, he said, "Well, my comments are just coming from my heart. I'm just saying what I feel."

I don't think he actually heard a difference between the articulate, fluent poem that he had written and recorded and his verbal comments. I asked, "What do you think the other students listening will think when they hear your recorded comment?"

"I think they will think that I'm a very intelligent, kind person," he answered.

"Okay, what do you think they will *hear*?" I asked, pushing for more precision.

"They will hear . . .," he hung his head in thought. "They will hear me saying 'hi' to my friends and trying real hard to speak clearly."

I paused and then asked, "What do you want them to hear?"

"I want them to hear me and think I'm smart because I am smart," he responded.

"You're right," I said. "How do you think you could show them that?"

"Hmm, maybe I could slow down and be careful how I say the words. I could probably only say the important things instead of my saying 'hi' to my friends."

"How could you do that?" I asked.

"Well, I could think about what I really want to say, practice it again, and then record," he offered.

After following his own plan, this student was able to record an understandable, fluent comment on VoiceThread. But I discovered it had to be *his* plan, not mine. For years, teachers had provided the steps for him to follow. It hadn't made any difference until he adopted the goals as his own and had a real reason to improve—in this case, other students who needed to understand his voice in order to understand his thoughts and ideas.

Grammar in Context

Another group that I targeted for differentiated instruction included students who were struggling with subject-verb agreement in writing and speaking, a very common difficulty in the community where I teach. Unfortunately, this is true not only outside the school walls but also within the school walls. Many teachers write off the vernacular as a regional or cultural dialect that simply is the way it is. I disagree and believe that teachers have a responsibility to guide students toward the Standard English practices that will enable them to succeed in college and careers. In my early years in teaching, I taught in an urban middle school where oral and written communication skills were disastrously weak; students wrote and spelled the way that they spoke. However, by teaching, modeling, reading, and expecting "professional" language at school, my colleagues and I were able to help the students distinguish between professional talk and home talk, which greatly improved their written and oral communication skills.

With this in mind, from the first day of school I expect students to answer all questions and make all comments in complete sentences, whether oral or written. Yes, it takes time to train students to answer in this way. But after a few weeks, the new practices become more habitual, until no one thinks about them anymore. In fact, students begin to police and correct one another. Of course, as with every lesson, some students need more reinforcement than others.

I gathered the students who still needed more support with subject-verb agreement and began our small-group discussion with a question: "Why do we need to learn proper grammar and mechanics?" This was not a new question for the students to contemplate. Throughout our lessons across content areas, I would ask similar questions that would cause them to pause and reflect upon the importance of what we were studying.

One of them responded, "We will need it for the future."

"In what way?" I asked.

Another student responded, "When we fill out a job application."

Another student interrupted, "Or for a job interview."

"I wonder why it would be important to use proper grammar in those situations," I mused.

One of them responded, "If you don't speak correctly, they will think that you are stupid and give the job to someone else."

"People will judge you and what you can do on their first impression," said another student.

"They will judge a book by its cover," said a third.

I pushed a little bit further, "Then what are some goals that we can make for our VoiceThread project?"

These students already had an understanding of their weaknesses and had set some goals in their previous writing projects. But as we continued our small-group discussion, they discovered that they all struggled with using correct subject-verb agreement, so they decided to set a new goal for improvement in the VoiceThread project.

We met at least once a day and used their poetry as a guide in lessons reviewing subject-verb agreement. We discussed how poetic license can cause a writer to occasionally suspend grammatical rules for the sake of the rhythm, rhyme, or meter. We also analyzed some of the resources on the topic of "going green" to find examples of correct subject and verb usage. When it came time to record and type their responses to other poems in the project, they often reminded and encouraged each other in their efforts. One student told me that if this had been a job interview, he would have gotten the position for sure. That spoke volumes to me: He understood the importance of proper grammar, he took pride in his work, and he thought about his audience while producing his work.

Igniting the Senses

I was able to differentiate instruction for yet another group during our VoiceThread project, this one involving students who had difficulty using descriptive words and figurative language in their writing. As I mentioned before, we are required to teach mode, not genre. Descriptive writing is one of those modes. Although the students had been using descriptive writing in different genres, several students were still struggling to paint a picture for the reader with their words.

Poetry was a great vehicle for practicing the use of descriptive writing. For these differentiated lessons, we analyzed the students' own poetry, their peers' poetry, and other poetry that we chose because it effectively appealed to the reader's five senses. Because we had studied figurative language in other lessons, this was not a new concept for them. However, while most of these students could identify examples of good figurative language within other texts, they could not extend that to their own writing.

"I wonder why it's important to include descriptive language in writing," I said.

They thought for a moment. With a question in her voice, one student answered, "It makes it sound better?"

"What do you mean by 'sounds better'?" I asked.

She pondered for a few moments. "'Sounds better' means that it has good words that kinda make it flow," she said.

Another student continued. "You know, it uses sound words, or smelling words, or seeing words."

I said, "I wonder why an author would do that."

One student jumped in: "An author uses those words so that the reader can see, feel, smell, or hear his writing."

I let the students think about that for a moment and then another a student added, "That means we need to use this in our writing, so our readers can use their senses to understand what we're writing better."

They had independently discovered the importance of using descriptive and figurative language: to better reach the audience with their word choice. This group continued to work on creating their poetry for the VoiceThread, selecting topics within our theme that most interested them.

As one student was composing her poem, she looked up at me and said, "I think it's important that the readers can hear the noise of the place that I'm writing about. They need to hear the beauty of nature so they'll want to protect it." When she finished writing, she read her poem out loud to our small group of students, and one of the other students commented, "Wow, that's a noisy poem." She grinned from ear to ear.

An Unquenchable Thirst

After the Jing experience, all of my students wanted to be involved in whatever tool or project a small group had initiated. They were always watching to see if they were going to miss out on something. They seemed to have one ear on what they were doing and one ear on what I was doing with another group. Many students asked to come before school or stay after school or do extra work at home in order to participate in the learning activities. They were so eager to learn and work. They often found it frustrating when an announcement would come on the intercom, a teacher would enter the room to ask me questions, or a change in the schedule caused us to curtail our classroom activities. My students had developed a real thirst for learning. Now I had to continue to find ways to quench that thirst each day with student-centered lessons supported by the new tools I was accumulating in my teaching toolbox.

Student Reflection

Jordan Beverly, fifth-grade student

VoiceThread was a new experience for me this year. VoiceThread is where you can create a slide show on any subject. Then, you can add your voice and later a lot of other people can make comments on your work. Before this year, I never knew something like this was even possible. I spend a lot of time at home on the computer, but VoiceThread was so much fun to work on. Mainly, I liked it because I had a great time working on a project that was really a group effort, not just your learning team, but the class and sometimes even people from across the country worked with you to make one amazing project.

CHAPTER

5

The Whole Is More Than the Sum of Its Parts

Standards and Skills

- Collaboration
- Expository writing
- Audience
- Technology operations and concepts
- Narrative writing

Technology Tools

- Lintor Make-A-Book (software and publishing materials)
- Wikis

My classroom, to the untrained eye, may look and sound chaotic. Students are noisily and busily engaged in learning through activities that stretch to every corner and often beyond the classroom borders. They debate, explain, justify, create, and communicate. And they are impatient with anything that distracts them from their purpose. As one student said after what seemed like the zillionth interruption of the day from the school office, "Mrs. Ramsay is all about business. We are all about business. Let us do our business!"

In a productive learning environment, there is no time to waste. Does this type of engagement magically happen? Of course not. Students in the intermediate grades need a tremendous amount of guidance that includes modeling, practicing, and reviewing.

Students must be involved in decision making and have choices so they will take ownership of the expectations, but the process involves a gradual release to freedom as they are able to handle greater levels of responsibility.

From the beginning of the year, I try to set the groundwork for a collaborative work environment. Notice that I did not say cooperative. Too often teachers incorrectly assume that the two words are synonyms for shared learning. Each term might have a place in our classrooms, but they do not have the same purpose.

I think my student Rachel explained it best: "The difference between cooperation and collaboration is that *cooperation* means everyone has the same goal and is doing the same job. If someone leaves, the job can still be done. *Collaboration* means that everyone has the same goal but they each are doing a different and important job; so if one was to leave, the job wouldn't get done."

Working Together to Learn

Throughout one year, I noticed that some of my students were still struggling with expository writing. They seemed to forget about the audience, making assumptions that the reader would understand their explanations. When I met individually with these students, they could usually, with some guidance and prompting, identify the crucial parts that they were leaving out of their writing. However, they continued to make the same types of mistakes when they returned to their work.

Targeting a small group of students for attention, I asked them to think of an activity from our class that they would like to share with their peers or families (not some mystery scorer) through their writing. They were interested in some of the space science and technology topics we were reviewing with our literature discussions of the novel *A Wrinkle in Time* (L'Engle 1962), but there were so many different ideas to consider that they couldn't decide which one to write about.

After listening to their discussion, I proposed that they write a how-to chapter book focusing on topics related to *A Wrinkle in Time*. They immediately agreed, and wondered if they could publish the book using our Lintor Make-A-Book software and publishing materials. "Can we make it a hardback book to share?" they asked.

Although we were gathered in the small-group area of the classroom while other students were busy with their individual or team tasks, I started to see all eyes focusing on us. Separate conversations quieted so they could hear our discussion. Hands from students in all other parts of the classroom started to go up. One by one they began offering suggestions for the nonfiction chapter book project. Before I knew it, someone had asked, "Can we work on it too?" What teacher could deny student requests to join in an extra writing activity? Definitely not me.

Getting Creative About Work Time

I divided the class into groups (sometimes pairs); each group would be responsible for a chapter. I took into consideration the interests of the writers as well as the skills I thought they could develop together. As had been our practice since the first day of school, each team member had a specific role to fulfill. The roles continued to rotate on a weekly basis.

Because of the district's pacing guides, we would have to find extra time in the school day to complete the chapter book project. I had to think creatively. We could use some of their language block/writing center time, but I also thought we might use the roughly twenty minutes at the beginning of the day that we typically allotted to housekeeping duties such as taking attendance and lunch count. Instead of our previous manual head counts, we began taking attendance and doing the lunch count using our interactive whiteboard. Students would come in, click in their attendance and lunch choice, and we would be done in a few minutes. The students directed the activity upon arrival, telling me who needed to be officially marked absent, and then they began working on their writing together. Once I had finished my morning duties, I would work with a group or two. (The first year that I did a project like this, I didn't teach math or science, except when they overlapped with the content that I was teaching in other subjects. However, when I became a self-contained fifth-grade teacher, I was also able to incorporate these types of projects into science and other content areas.)

Another option that my excited authors suggested was that we "skip lunch" in order to keep writing. Often, we would be working on their writing projects and they would be frustrated because they had to stop to go to another class or location, such as the cafeteria. Of course, they weren't really suggesting that they wouldn't eat lunch. Instead, they wanted to bring lunch back to the classroom so that they could continue to work on their writing, free from the noise in the lunchroom. They would get their food, return to the classroom, continue their writing until the end of lunchtime, and return their trays and trash to the cafeteria. This gave them an additional twenty to thirty minutes of time to work together.

Because we already had so much going on in our school day in addition to the students collaboratively writing this chapter book, we did not create a formal rubric. Also, our school district specifies exactly how many and which

FIGURE 5.1

Expository Chapter Checklist

_____   Explanation/information about _____

_____   Introduction: connection to *A Wrinkle in Time*

_____   Steps explaining "how-to"

_____   Transition words (for example: *first, second, then, next, finally*, etc.)

_____   Text that is understandable for audience

_____   COPS used for editing (See Figure 1.1)

_____   Examples, charts, illustrations, photos to help audience's understanding

_____   Final chapter published in software

assignments must be graded during a given period, so it is not always feasible for us to create a rubric and get a fully graded piece every time we write. Instead, the students suggested that they develop a checklist to help keep everyone on task for this chapter book project (see Figure 5.1). Box 5.1 describes another option for tracking student progress, the class "war board."

Box 5.1 Tracking Student Progress with a War Board

One task completion method that I've used is a war board. Some students find it easier to see their name moving from one step to the next on a physical space. We variously take a section of our whiteboard, interactive whiteboard, or chart paper, break down each step of the project, and create categories (brainstorming, editing, waiting to conference, etc.) on the war board. Students then move their names under the appropriate category each day, depending on what they are cur- rently working on. Often students who are ahead of the rest of the class voluntarily assist their peers. I discovered that whenever we didn't create a war board or some sort of device to keep everyone on task, some of my writers would ask for a piece of large art paper and create one for the class on their own. Their peers would go to them and move their names along the list. The key with these methods is that students create them and monitor their own progress.

Thinking About the Audience

To assign chapters for our chapter book project, I grouped students with similar individual writing goals and interests, and I guided them toward an appropriate chapter. For example, I matched students from the original group that needed help communicating with the audience in expository writing with chapters that focused on step-by-step explanations. One of these chapters had to do with a science experiment that they had conducted in class. As they prepared to write "How to Build a Robot Arm," I noticed that they were omitting several steps, making assumptions that the audience would understand their meaning. I asked Robert to explain the experiment to me.

"Well," he said, "first in this experiment, you have to get your robot arm and try picking up a marker. Then you try to pick up a pencil. After that you try to pick up a paper clip. Finally, you write down your results and your final conclusions."

"Okay," I said. "Does anyone else have something that you want to add to Robert's explanation?"

"No, I think that covers it," Kate answered.

"All right, then I would like for Sarah to stand up and follow just the directions that Robert gave. Robert, would you repeat those directions?"

He nodded and began, "First, you need to get your robot arm and try to pick up a marker."

Sarah looked around and said, "Where's the robot arm? Oh, I'll go get ours."

I looked at them and they looked at each other. "Uh-oh. I forgot to tell how to make a robot arm," Robert realized.

Rebecca spoke up, "We're also going to need a marker."

"Hmm, I wonder what we could do about that," I said.

Sarah replied, "Well, I could go and get all of the supplies before Robert tells me what I need to do."

Robert agreed, and they began creating a list of all the materials for the job.

"So you're creating a list of supplies. Why?" I asked.

Sarah explained, "Well, we're creating a list because I need to know what I'll need before we begin."

I pushed for deeper thinking.

"If Robert were the author in this scenario that we're acting out, what role would Sarah have?" I asked. "Who is she in the writing process?" Confused looks. "If Robert were the only person writing this chapter, what's Sarah job?" More thinking.

Robert hesitantly replied, "Sarah is the person who is supposed to follow my directions."

"If Sarah is supposed to follow your directions, what does that mean for Robert?" I questioned.

Rebecca answered, "That means that Robert has to tell her everything that she needs to do or she can't do it. Like, when he told her to use her robot arm. Sarah didn't have one because he didn't tell her how to make one first and she didn't have the marker because he didn't tell her to get one first."

A chorus of "ohs" escaped their lips. They were starting to see the role of their writing for their audience. This type of discussion occurred with several of the groups as they wrote. Sometimes they would grasp the idea without having to act it out, but often the dramatic reenactment helped them to see what they were missing in their writing.

Publishing Our Project

Each small group worked on a different chapter. The purpose, to explain or inform about a classroom activity, was a common thread throughout all chapters. In addition, the members of each group had to work together and depend on one another to be successful. Collaboratively, they brainstormed, wrote, edited, revised, and published their individual chapters. When teams had completed their chapters, the students would volunteer to work on another part of the chapter book, such as the cover or title page, using Lintor Make-A-Book materials (as described in Chapter 2). Later we also published their writing to our class Web site for friends and family to view and enjoy. (See www.ramsaysclass.com/WrinkleHow-to.htm for their final product.)

Same Strategy, Different Mode

Building on the success of the collaborative writing and publishing, I hoped to keep the momentum going using a similar project to deepen students' understanding of the narrative writing mode. I had several students who always struggled when trying to create an interesting story with the required elements of character, plot, setting, and problem and solution. Narrative writing—telling a story—is something that most students have done since they were very young. However, I found that my students' plots lacked sequential content and the problem-solution composition that makes for mature, interesting writing. I noticed that they also typically left out key descriptive elements that help readers visualize the story.

A little voice in the back of my head kept telling me that I should focus on drilling those skills for standardized testing, as I had done in previous years. Although I reminded myself that my students were growing at a much faster rate across all content areas with more contextual instruction, I still had some doubt about whether this new focus would still prepare my learners for the upcoming state testing cycle. By this point, at the beginning of the second semester in the school year, we had taken several assessments to predict their success on the standardized tests. My students had scored well on those tests, better than previous students in previous years. My current students' writing for prompts or open-ended questions on practice tests had quickly improved as well. With those benchmarks as reassurance, I stayed on the new path and began searching for another technology-assisted activity that could sharpen my students' narrative writing skills.

In the past, I had used an activity called a Writing Roulette. This is how it works: One student begins writing a story (usually with a provided prompt, which can involve any content area) for five minutes and then passes it off to the next student. The second student then reads what was written and spends seven minutes editing and adding to the story. The process continues until everyone in the group has had the opportunity to contribute to the story. Students tend to be more careful with their writing because they know a peer will be reading and analyzing it. I had always had success with this project, but I wanted to expand it to bring in the dimensions of a larger audience and the state standards in writing, grammar, and mechanics.

Through an ISTE webinar, I discovered a collaborative tool called a wiki, which enables multiple people in different locations to collaborate on one document or collection of work. Among the many different providers available, I chose to use Wikispaces (www.wikispaces.com). (Box 5.2 provides some tips for getting started with wikis.)

Knowing how much my students loved writing for and with other students, I invited the teacher of the class with whom my students had been writing e-pal letters to participate. We began planning for our two classes to create a collaborative story with multiple authors.

And Away We Go

After setting up our wiki, I helped my students determine the parameters that we would use for equitable access to the Writing Roulette. Using data from previous assessments, both formal and informal, I gave priority to students who were struggling with narrative writing and/or grammar and mechanics. These students were given scheduled time every day to work on the wiki, whereas the rest of the class might only do so once or twice a week.

Devante suggested that students work no longer than five minutes at a time so everyone would have the opportunity to add to the wiki each day.

Box 5.2 Wiki, Wiki

Appropriately named for the Hawaiian word *wiki*, which means "fast," this tool is indeed quick and simple. Creating a wiki is fairly intuitive. After visiting the Web site (in my case, www.wikispaces .com), you sign up, register an e-mail address, and start creating.

There are various restrictions you can set up for your wiki. You can create a wiki that the general public can view and edit. You can also choose to let the public view the wiki, but not edit it; with this option, someone has to make a request through the wiki and get approval from the creator (which was me, in this case) to make edits. I chose the second option because it met all of my criteria: free, viewable by friends and family, and safe for my students.

Wikispaces offers K–12 teachers a free upgrade that is ad-free and comes with some added features (go to this URL for the upgrade: www.wikispaces.com/site/for/teachers). With this upgrade, teachers can go to the User Creator tool under the Manage Wiki option on the toolbar and set up accounts for their students in bulk, even when students do not have e-mail addresses. This enables students to not only upload and edit content on the wikis but also participate in discussion boards that are available for the approved users on each page.

I also discovered instructional videos on YouTube that demonstrate the how-to's of technology applications. At the YouTube site, you can type "wiki tutorial" (or another Web 2.0 application) in the Search box. Common Craft offers some of the easiest tutorials to understand and follow. I discovered Common Craft videos on YouTube, but you can locate all of their tutorials on their Web site (www.commoncraft.com). Similar sites, such as TeacherTube (www1 .teachertube.com), may have the same tutorials and usually are not blocked by district firewalls. The tutorials are free—welcome news for all of us on tight budgets.

"But what if it takes you five minutes to just read the story?" Rachel asked. "You wouldn't have time to make any additions to the story. You have to have time to actually think about what you are reading so that what you add makes the story better."

Devante agreed and suggested fifteen minutes per turn, which appealed to his peers. Unlike the previous publishing ventures, this activity required students to take turns instead of collaborating simultaneously on their writing. We used the built-in, thirty-minute center time during reading class to work on the wiki and rotated so that each team had dedicated access to the wiki during the week.

I then shared the criteria with my partner teacher. Together we set a rough, two-week deadline for this writing project. This was a "by invitation only" wiki—that is, only students in our two classes could access it—so that we could both closely monitor what was being created and meet the safety needs of our schools.

As usual, I had to "borrow" time to complete the project. Many of the students whom I had targeted for assistance arrived on the early buses before school began so I could work with them directly. Most of them just needed more practice and encouragement that their writing was a valuable part of the class story.

Assessing Collaborative Publishing

We did not formally grade this activity with a rubric, due to time constraints, but we did evaluate it. One feature of the wiki that I particularly like is being able to track the editing. By clicking on the History tab at the top of a page, you can see the list of edits by name, time, and date. By clicking on the date and author, you can see the insertions highlighted in green and the deletions in red. This feature automatically gives you a record of each student's progress, a very handy tool when differentiating instruction. Instead of waiting until the end of the project, I was able to conference with the learners throughout. I met with the targeted students several times a week.

Because we were preparing for the upcoming standardized writing assessment, we focused on improving our narrative writing by adding sequential transition words and vivid verbs, adjectives, and vocabulary. The students brainstormed a list of criteria and guidelines for the wiki project:

- All additions and deletions should improve the meaning of the story or correct grammatical errors, because errors keep the reader from understanding the text.
- The first thing that each writer must do is to read and make additions or corrections to previously written text, focusing on vivid verbs, transition words, and vocabulary.
- No student can add more than a paragraph a day.
- Students can collaborate and discuss their writing in pairs or groups of three during their individual turns at the computer.
- Each writer must respect anything created by another student.

Putting It into Practice

Because much of the writing occurred during center time when I was working with small groups, I observed from the back of the classroom until I looked at the wiki history after school. I noticed that my students gravitated toward working in pairs, and they were often so excited about what they had written that they couldn't wait to share it with me or their peers.

By happenstance, we discovered that only one pair at one school could work on our single wiki page at a time. When groups of students at our two school locations were online simultaneously, the last saved version erased the other pair's work. Due to the time zone difference between the schools, we were able to avoid this problem between classes. The most important aspect of dealing with this issue was that students found the potential problem and they aided in discovering the solution. We stumbled a bit together; we solved the problem together; we grew together.

One day, I noticed three students involved in some heated negotiations. Priscilla informed me that she had already used her allotted time on the wiki but needed more. Her writing partner, Mayda, had space in her schedule but she wanted to continue writing with a different partner. Priscilla was flummoxed. "Mrs. Ramsay, I have to write it now," she implored. "I'm going to forget it if I don't get it down right now!" I asked them what they thought would be a fair way to make that happen. The girls agreed to rotate partners, and Priscilla jotted her ideas so she wouldn't forget them while waiting for her next turn.

The amazing thing is that these students had been my most hesitant writers before the project began. Other students engaged in similar negotiations over time (trying to work the system) and word choices (should we use *beautiful* or *spectacular*?). My students frequently requested, and later begged for, more time to read, edit, and write.

By using a wiki instead of the traditional Writing Roulette, sixty-four students contributed to our final product. They wrote and edited it following the directions and staying within the parameters of the narrative mode. The wiki enabled students to immediately see the changes and discuss how their writing or a peer's writing affected the story progression or the final outcome. Instead of the traditional sequence of first draft, editing, and rewriting, students had the power to create a "working version" of their story, which gave them the time to make thoughtful choices. I realized that I had harnessed something that today's students crave—immediacy of feedback and results.

To see the students' final product, visit http://fesoeswritingroulette .wikispaces.com/An+Accidental+Discovery.

Wikis in the Classroom

A wiki can work in a classroom that has only one computer with Internet access, which was where I started. In subsequent years I acquired six classroom computers by writing grants, talking to area business owners, and stressing the importance of preparing students for the future to our school administration. With these additional resources my students spend more time writing and less time waiting to write.

We currently use wikis for two ongoing projects. Because many of the state science standards are not addressed in our fifth-grade text, I created one wiki for our science class (http://ramsayscience5.wikispaces.com/). Not only can I provide extra resources in different learning modalities through the use of this wiki, but the students also create content for each of the science units. Parents love that they can view the wiki and guide their children at home in preparation for assessment.

Our other ongoing project, The Coast to Coast Chronicles, is an online journal created by students across the country (www.ramsaysclass.com/collaboration_station.htm). The wiki is an excellent way for students in multiple locations to compile their writing projects for easy access. Each edition has a different theme, selected by the students, which drives their writing.

After we published one of the editions of The Coast to Coast Chronicles, students from our partner schools asked in a Moodle post how we came up with such clever and cool writing ideas. Brooke responded to them: "We had twenty-five brains working together coming up with ideas. That's much stronger than just one brain."

Wikis are an extremely versatile tool to implement, regardless of age group or content area, because students can be in the same physical classroom or on the other side of the world working and writing collaboratively. Here are a few other suggested applications for wikis:

- In a math class, students can create problems and have other students respond with a written solution.
- Students can collaborate on a class constitution or create project guidelines.
- Students can maintain a class, schoolwide, or district wiki newsletter.
- Students can brainstorm ideas to solve social, ecological, or cultural challenges in their communities and debate the advantages or disadvantages of various solutions.
- Students can submit portfolios of their work, which are open to feedback from their peers.
- Students can discuss literature, similar to a book chat or literature circle. The prompts can be student driven or teacher driven, depending on the age, content, or ability level of the learners.
- Students can submit journal entries for a historical figure or time period, which requires them to think from another point of view.
- Students can submit lab reports, observations, and conclusions based on hands-on experiences and research about a scientific principle.
- Students can compose a cross-curriculum journal of varied modes of writing based on a central theme, idea, or concept.

Open-Ended Collaboration

Through collaborative projects, writing in my classroom became much more than the traditional exercises in grammar and mechanics. My students learned to love writing because it helped them communicate and make thoughtful, respectful additions to a collaborative project for an authentic audience. Students spent much of their time discussing and sometimes debating the virtues of their ideas, which demonstrated higher-order critical thinking. My students wanted to bounce ideas off one another, always seeking justification of why those ideas were necessary to the final outcome. As a result, much more thoughtful writing ensued.

My students still write collaboratively, but now our projects typically involve their peers from many states. Although we continue to publish some books for our classroom, we have moved to creating content online through tools such as wikis and VoiceThread (see Chapter 4) in order to make the writing accessible to our many out-of-state writing partners. These tools enable authors from various locations with different types of equipment and ability levels to create and communicate together, working toward a common goal.

Previously my students would roll their eyes and sigh when I mentioned a writing assignment. Now they are enthusiastic, particularly when they get to explain something (key to expository writing) or tell a story (key to narrative writing), incorporating what they've learned and enjoyed. I realized how much my role as a teacher had changed when a colleague described my classroom this way: "The students are driving the train. You're just navigating in the background to make sure it doesn't derail." How wonderful, I thought. Just watch us go, full steam ahead!

CHAPTER

6

Stepping Back in Time

F ired up by the success of previous writing projects, my students were always asking, "What's next?" After publishing their digital stories, they were particularly eager to try something new and ambitious in our social studies class. Using sophisticated metacognitive skills, they realized that they learned and retained more when they could connect the content to their lives.

Several students expressed an interest in creating historical fiction that could address our social studies standards while giving them additional practice in narrative writing. It was thrilling as a teacher to recognize that my students were searching for ways to extend their writing across the curriculum. As usual, I had to think quickly to stay ahead of their accelerated learning agenda.

Standards and Skills
- Writing historical fiction
- Audience
- Cause-effect and choice-consequence relationships
- Literary elements and devices
- Technology operations and concepts
- Compare and contrast

Technology Tools
- Microsoft PowerPoint (software)
- SimplyBox (http://simplybox.com)
- Edmodo (www.edmodo.com)
- MyPodcast (www.mypodcast.com)
- Audacity (software)

Same Tool, Different Use

Sometimes we are drawn to the flashier technology tools that have the most potential for generating "wow" responses from students. However, I have found that by rethinking the application of familiar tools, we can often find simple and effective methods for encouraging young authors to write and think creatively. The other benefit to a low-frills approach is being able to circumvent limitations in technology resources.

When I taught the middle grades at an urban school, I had few computers and no Internet access. Our computers did have the Microsoft Office suite, so I tried to think of inventive ways to use the software. One tool that I employed to good effect was Microsoft PowerPoint. Now, I know that in this day and age, many people consider PowerPoint an outdated, passive computer software application. Most of us have seen too many people "kill" their audiences by reading long, boring PowerPoint presentations, which really defeats the purpose of having a speaker. "Just give us the presentation," we want to shout in frustration. "We all know how to read."

There is a much more audience-friendly way to use PowerPoint. Although many of us think of hyperlinks as quick clicks to an outside Web site, in PowerPoint the hyperlink function also lets you jump to a different slide within a presentation. That means that instead of a linear format, where slide 2 follows slide 1, and so on, a user can insert a hyperlink button and move to any other place in the presentation.

Linking this feature to my literacy lessons, I was able to envision a new role for PowerPoint. Many of my students love the Choose Your Own Adventure book series, which lets readers select the plot sequence. At climactic transitions, these books offer readers a list of options for the next step. Readers choose an option and turn to the specified page to find out how the story will continue. Choose Your Own Adventure stories help readers make predictions and become more involved in the story. I have also found that students tend to reread these books, making different choices each time through.

I could see how, using the hyperlinks feature in PowerPoint, my students could create their own adventure stories with varied plot twists, giving readers of their work opportunities to make predictions and choices. This seemed like a happy combination of reading and writing skills with the support of a simple technology tool.

My idea was to have the students create historical fiction stories based on the Great Depression, the time period we were studying. We were already reading *Bud, Not Buddy*, the popular book by Christopher Paul Curtis (2002) set in the 1930s, and we had previously read other historical fiction, such as

Island of the Blue Dolphins, so I knew that my students had some knowledge of the genre. They would be able to write historical fiction using PowerPoint and inserting hyperlinks so that readers could choose different plot paths.

I had two major goals for this project. First, I wanted students to understand the time period and the choices and consequences that Americans faced during the Great Depression. Second, I wanted to give my struggling readers another way to identify and practice cause and effect, an important literacy skill that prepares them for academic writing commonly found in history and science texts.

Becoming Genre Experts

As usual, my students were wildly enthusiastic about trying this new writing project. To enhance their background knowledge while reading *Bud, Not Buddy,* we had already explored America's Great Depression through primary source documents, videos, and guest speakers. Recognizing the historical importance of radio broadcasts, which President Franklin Roosevelt used when speaking to Americans about Depression-era issues such as the banking crisis, New Deal legislation, and the reorganization of the nation's judiciary, we had also listened to his fireside chats and other early "wireless" communications. Now, with a boost from contemporary technology, my students seized the chance to write historical fiction that would bring this dark period in our nation's past to life.

We started by reading widely in the genre of historical fiction. I found many samples through my personal reading and by asking teachers in my PLN, which includes several media specialists who are experts at locating samples of different genres online (see Box 6.1 for tips). Working in teams, students identified and analyzed the characteristics of historical fiction, which evolved into a checklist to guide the writing and publishing of their stories. (See Box 6.2 for more information about effective ways to organize data for writing projects in any genre.)

They determined that historical fiction should include these characteristics:

- Realistic characters, whether they are real or fictional
- Dialogue that enhances the story and can illustrate characters, tell about beliefs/thoughts of that time period, or explain events going on
- An authentic setting for the time period of the story
- A problem for the characters to solve that is realistic to the time period
- Characters making choices with consequences (cause-effect)

- Plots that may include a mix of historical and fictional events
- A believable solution at the end
  (*Note:* After they wrote their Choose Your Own Adventure stories, the students created another list [see page 93] to guide the publication.)

Box 6.1 | **Locating Genre Samples**

When searching for good samples of genre writing for my students to read and analyze, I often begin with local newspapers and then progress to larger publications such as *The Miami Herald* or *The New York Times*. Reviewing the online databases, I try to select articles, reviews, or opinion pieces with current topics that will appeal to my students.

For genres such as historical fiction, science fiction, or nonfiction, I refer to a large collection of books that I have built over the years to supplement social studies texts. Students need to be able to read several samples of the genre we are reviewing and then discuss and analyze the common characteristics. Because of our ever-present time constraints, picture books and excerpts of lengthier books are often excellent choices for our studies.

One Web-based resource that I've discovered is Lit2Go (http://etc.usf.edu/lit2go/). It is a free, online collection of stories and poems that are available not only in print but also in MP3 format. You can search the database by author, title, subject matter, or reading level. Then you can view the text as a Web page or a pdf file; you can also open iTunes and listen to the MP3 version of the story or poem.

For books that cut across fictional genres and student ability levels, I often visit Children's Storybooks Online at www.magickeys.com/books/#ya. For samples of folklore, I recommend the American Folklore site at www.americanfolklore.net.

Box 6.2 | **Collect, Analyze, and Share Writing Samples Using SimplyBox**

Using technology, it is easier than ever to collect well-written samples of any genre you may teach. One common tool that I have used more and more over the years is SimplyBox (www.simplybox.com). This bookmarking service enables you to take screen shots of Web sites and place them in different boxes or categories. I usually create boxes for fables, letters, articles, PSAs, free verse poetry, historical fiction, or whatever we are working on at the time. All my genre boxes are placed in a "container" I name Writing Samples. I usually find representative works from authors who have published their writing online.

Each time I find something relevant, I "box it" and drag it to the appropriate genre category.

SimplyBox lets you keep the material private, share it with certain users you invite through e-mail, or make it public. Each of the boxes gets its own URL.

My students like SimplyBox because they can see a miniature version of the Web site that they want to visit on the SimplyBox page before they click on it. They can access the writing samples throughout the project. And they can comment on the Web pages housed in SimplyBox as well as see the observations and comments from their peers.

Organizational Strategies

To make the Choose Your Own Adventure historical fiction writing project manageable, my students suggested that they all use a similar plot pattern (either choice-consequence or cause-effect, common devices in historical writing) with a limited number of plot choices. They wanted to ensure that readers could make good predictions about the resolution of the stories without having to pursue too many confusing paths.

Based on their prior knowledge of historical writing, my authors reminded each other that while the story may be fictitious, the historical information used in the fiction had to be accurate and realistic. They created the following list to guide the publication of the project:

- Total of eight slides
- Title slide on slide 1
- Opening scenario on slide 2 with two hyperlink choices
- Each of those first two choices would have two more hyperlink choices
- Font and background should make it easy for a reader to read
- Illustrations should enhance the story, providing support for the text

Due to our time limitations, the students agreed that they would write in teams. They seemed to have a clear view of what they needed to accomplish, so I let them begin their prewriting. I moved from team to team, listening to their ideas as they brainstormed the settings, characters, and plots. Because many students got caught up in one story line without thinking about the alternative choices, I spent more time than usual conferencing with each group to guide them back to where they needed to be. Consequently, I wasn't getting to see every team as often as I usually do during a collaborative writing project.

After a couple of days, it was as if the lid had come off their blenders: We had stories with no endings, parts without the main characters, and story lines that made no sense. One student looked up at me and said, "Um, Mrs. Ramsay. We really created a huge mess. How will we ever clean this up?" It was time to step back and begin again.

This was an ambitious writing project. My students weren't just writing an imaginative story set in a historic time period. They also had to weave their characters into four different plot choices. After working with the groups over two days, I realized they were having trouble "seeing" the different story lines. We decided to create a simple graphic organizer (see Figure 6.1) to sort out the pieces of the wonderfully complicated stories they had imagined. This graphic organizer, created in Microsoft Word, helped my students keep track of their prewriting and planning. Different hyperlink buttons (represented by the arrows on the chart) would continue the story based on the reader's choices. Students can use a printed form like the one shown in Figure 6.1 or they can draw their own graphic organizers.

Over the years I've tried several different ways of guiding students through the planning stage of the Choose Your Own Adventure story project. We used Inspiration/Webspiration (a collaborative mapping or planning online tool) when I had a free trial version of the software. But after the trial period ended, I didn't have money to purchase a license so we moved on to another method. However, this is a useful tool that you may want to investigate to assist your students in planning a story.

During prewriting students wanted enough space on the graphic organizer to add details of the plot and the cause-effect relationships. We discovered that

FIGURE 6.1

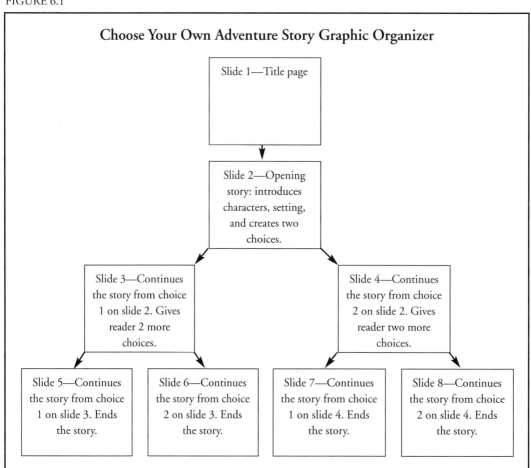

| Box 6.3 | **Edmodo: Another Way to Boost Instructional Time** |

Edmodo (www.edmodo.com) is a Web site that lets teachers post assignments, polls, and alerts and send them to individual students or a selected a group. You can also upload files and add them to your project library as well as set due dates for assignments.

When students log in to Edmodo, they can see and complete the assignments digitally. Teachers can provide private comments on the assignments and post grades for each student.

Edmodo gives me more time to work directly with my students so I can spend less time grading papers. If we are running short on time in class, students can electronically submit graphic organizers or other checkpoint features of a project to let me know they are on track. I can write comments after class and then we can discuss them the next day if necessary.

---

the best organizing method was a low-tech option: cutting their lined notebook paper in half to represent each of the numbered boxes. We've tried other methods in addition to Inspiration/Webspiration, but students keep migrating back to this simple collating technique. I think they enjoy the tangible quality of being able to physically lay out their stories and see how they will connect before using PowerPoint and the hyperlink buttons. Often I would see team members spread out in the floor, bent over the story layouts as they discussed the additions they wanted to make.

Recently our school purchased portable netbooks. With additional computers at their disposal, my students can accomplish more of their prewriting and planning in a digital format. See Box 6.3 for more information.

Our Own Fireside Chats

Toward the end of the Choose Your Own Adventure historical fiction project, several students approached me with a collective brainstorm: In addition to using PowerPoint to enhance their historical fiction, they also wanted to use podcasts to create radio broadcasts to bring more historical realism to this unit on the Great Depression. Before I could ask them to explain, they immediately started supporting their plan.

"Mrs. Ramsay, we know that it has to have social studies and writing content," one of the students said, no doubt thinking about all the times we had linked our work to the content standards for each subject.

"It can't be just fun," another student interrupted. "It has to make us better learners."

"Right," the first student said, jumping back into the conversation, "it has to help us communicate to our audience too, making them think."

I got goose bumps hearing my students analyze their learning this way. They had drawn on their previous experience with e-pals, when they had communicated information to a real audience in a lively format. They had recognized the historical importance of radio broadcasts and conceived a contemporary twist. They had also realized that strong writing is the foundation of all communication. Moreover, they had internalized my mantra that technology must aid or supplement learning, not distract from it. They fully demonstrated the ISTE NETS for Students 1, Creativity and Innovation.

Their marvelous insights—and so many others that continue to pop up in our classroom conversations to this day—give me the energy to overcome the obstacles of implementing technology in public schools. Every blocked Web site, malfunctioning piece of equipment, and overbooked chunk of instructional time is just an unfortunate interference. With happy and excited learners in the back of my mind, there is always some way to overcome these obstacles for the greater good of students.

Because we were already struggling to find time to complete the Create Your Own Adventure stories, I offered the Great Depression radio program podcast as an extra activity for any students who finished early. The students could work with their historical fiction groups or choose to work with other partners or alone. Despite the rapid pace, many students chose to participate in the second project and were almost exuberant about the additional work they had agreed to do.

As I reflected on their greater enthusiasm for this second project, I realized a subtle difference. While the first project was prompted by students who wanted to write historical fiction, I ended up doing most of the instruction, showing them how to write the twisting plot sequences and create an appealing, interactive digital presentation with PowerPoint. By contrast, the radio podcast was their brainchild. As author and digital education expert Bernajean Porter says:

Allowing students to choose their own types, modes, and tools as well as to personally select the assessment indicators that you will use to evaluate their digital work increases student ownership, affinity, and independent learning skills. We want students to become designers of learning tasks and consumers of assessment information and take responsibility for using evidence of their own progress to understand what comes next for them. (2010, 16)

I definitely saw this pride in ownership play out in my classroom with these two historically based writing activities.

Putting Technology in Their Toolboxes

How do teachers and students know what technology tools are appropriate for a given writing project? I often let students explore different tools that I have heard about or used and we discuss the benefits and drawbacks for our current writing project.

I also let students see projects that previous classes have created. Because all of the work is housed on my class Web site, it's easy to provide time at the beginning of the school year to show students the myriad projects, tools, and opportunities that lay ahead of them. That said, we do not do the same projects from year to year because students make most of the choices about what they will write and how they will communicate and publish.

Where the Past Meets the Present

As the students discussed what needed to be included in their podcasts, one theme continued to dominate their conversations. Just as the historical fiction made choice-consequence and cause-effect connections for readers, the podcast authors thought that their audience needed to understand the similarities and differences between entertainment in Depression-era America and entertainment today. They kept repeating, "This can't just be a fun program. That's too easy. It has to teach something."

The irony that they were re-creating an entertainment medium from the past with the technology tools of today was not lost on them. In the end, the students chose to record their writing as podcasts that implied a comparison/contrast to modern entertainment. Their goal was to produce a "radio show" that had some similarities to modern comedies, dramas, or news broadcasts seen online or on television but used a communications medium that was more popular in the past.

Like digital stories, we use podcasts in multiple ways to support writing each school year. The first year that we decided to try podcasts, I searched for a user-friendly, free tool. I had attended a workshop where MyPodcast (www.mypodcast.com) was mentioned. It was very straightforward to use. After setting up an account and downloading the free software, you use the recording device similar to the way you would use an old cassette tape player. When the recording is complete, you click to publish, and the software converts the file and uploads it for podcast listeners. MyPodcast requires users to include an advertisement, but you can choose where the ad appears. We always included it at the end of each podcast.

After the first year of using MyPodcast, I wanted to keep the podcasts on our class Web site instead of online, so we searched for a different podcast production method. Today we use Audacity (http://audacity.sourceforge.net), which includes a free audio recorder as well as editing software. Audacity has a multitude of functions and tools so students can edit their voice tracks and add music. Once a project is completed in Audacity, you can export it as a WAV file or an MP3 file. Those formats are easy to upload to a Web site, an MP3 player, or a wiki to share with your audience.

Leave It to My Students

The first time we used Audacity, I downloaded the program to my laptop at home, but I didn't have time to figure out the features and anticipate the problems. I knew my students were going to be taking a districtwide test that day, so I thought I would have time to investigate Audacity during the test. Much to my surprise, Brooke had a different idea when she met me before school.

"Mrs. Ramsay," she said, "I could look at it and see if I can figure it out, if that's okay." I handed the laptop off to her. Within ten minutes, she had figured out how to record, add music, edit parts in or out of the recording, fade music in and out at the beginning or end of the podcast, and alter the sound level of each of the different tracks. Then Brooke asked if it would be okay to set up the laptop and record her own podcast. I was so amazed at her confidence. She wasn't afraid that she wouldn't be able to figure out this new software; she was sure that she could!

Because we were recording so often to complete digital stories, VoiceThread projects, and podcasts, it had become disruptive to keep silencing the classroom each time students needed to go into broadcast mode. Luckily they found a solution. They converted a large storage room next to our classroom into a sound booth. The storage room has no heating, air-conditioning, or intercoms, which means no distracting noises to interfere with the recordings. The room also has no electrical outlets, but students found an extension cord and linked it from the laptop to the nearest outlet in the hallway. By 10 o'clock that morning, Brooke had orchestrated the recording of a third of her classmates' podcasts just before the testing was to begin. Within three days, she had guided everyone through the production phase.

New Level of Learning

As my learners were creating their Choose Your Own Adventure stories and Depression-era radio show podcasts, I realized how much they had matured as writers, collaborators, and communicators, but also in terms of their confidence, problem solving, and higher-level thinking skills. The next year, a sixth-grade teacher told me that my students had a deep understanding of the Great Depression and were enthusiastic about sharing their knowledge. She said she was amazed that in addition to knowing basic facts about the time period, my former students had empathy for the hardships that their ancestors had experienced and a rich perspective of the impact of choices and consequences in history.

Her comments validated my decision to devote time to our collaborative writing and publishing projects. And her feedback also reinforced the value of what author and educator Rick Wormeli defines as "mastery" learning:

> *Students have mastered content when they demonstrate a thorough understanding as evidenced by doing something substantive with the content beyond merely echoing it. Anyone can repeat information; it's the masterful student who can break content into its component pieces, explain it and alternative perspectives regarding it cogently to others, and use it purposefully in new situations.* (2006, 12)

Our historical writing projects gave my students the opportunity to share and apply their research about the time period with an authentic audience—other learners in our school and across the country. They went much further than just spitting out some facts that didn't mean anything to them. By writing complex historical fiction, they had to place themselves in the Depression mindset and think about choices and consequences. They had to think about how life had changed for them as a result of decisions others made in previous generations and realize that without knowledge of the past, history really could repeat itself. Many of my learners expressed gratitude for what they have today: the comforts of home, three meals a day, toys and entertainment, an education, and a bright future. The historical fiction project and the radio show podcast project brought the students face to face with the realities and possibilities of life.

My student authors had also reached a new level of learning using technology to support their education. They saw a challenge and tackled it wholeheartedly. They searched for new ways to write, share their vision, and connect with content in order to teach others. Bernajean Porter advises, "Whatever tools you use, putting the priority on rigor and fluency of the modes will benefit students long after tools become obsolete or new tools become available" (2010, 16).

As Jordan, one of my previously hesitant writers, told me, "Mrs. Ramsay, I've decided I really like to write. I just prefer a keyboard to a pencil. It's easier to say what I want to say to my audience and share all my ideas. Do you think it would be possible for me to come back next year and work with your students, teaching them how to write?"

A student as a teacher? Absolutely! Who better to help encourage and teach my future writers?

(For examples of the Choose Your Own Adventure stories and radio show podcasts mentioned in this chapter, see www.stenhouse.com/skiplunch.)

CHAPTER
7

Passion and Persuasion

Standards and Skills
- Persuasive writing
- Communication: written and oral
- Digital citizenship
- Audience

Technology Tools
- Skype (www.skype.com/intl/en-us/home)
- SimplyBox (http://simplybox.com/)
- YouTube (www.youtube.com) and TeacherTube (www1.teachertube.com)
- Zamzar (www.zamzar.com)

I n forty minutes, we're going live!" Matthew said, sounding like a television emcee.

"I know. I hope I don't forget what I've written," Rachel said. "I wanted to memorize it so that they wouldn't be distracted by me holding my paper."

Elizabeth chimed in, "I can't believe we're going to be able to talk to students on the other side of the country and actually see them. You know, without being *with* them."

"I'm nervous," Priscilla added. The others nodded their heads in agreement.

After months of communicating with other students only through their writing, my excited and anxious students were about to meet them face-to-face in our first class experiment with Skype. The project: persuasive writing as performance.

New Inspiration

As adults, much of what we read and often what we write is persuasive in nature, trying to convince someone to take action or to agree with our opinions. Today, with the ease of accessing the Internet and Web 2.0 tools with laptops, smart phones, or tablets, people are able to voice their outrage and call for change for anything from poor customer service at a local store to animal cruelty. Most of us understand that to get our point across, we must carefully choose our wording and remain calm and professional while giving plenty of support to defend our positions.

Students also are inundated with examples of persuasive writing—whether on the radio or television, in a magazine, or on their favorite fan Web site. But they typically have little experience analyzing and applying the techniques of persuasive writing. Anticipating that I would need to address not only the state standard where students must master writing a persuasive text, including a minimum of three reasons to support the writer's position (Alabama State Department of Education 2007), but also the NCTE/IRA (1996) Standards 4 (dealing with spoken, written, and visual language) and 5 (dealing with writing process elements), I searched for a new approach to teaching persuasive writing.

My students had created a wide range of writing samples within the three modes (narrative, descriptive, and expository) tested on Alabama's fifth-grade assessment. But after the state test at the end of February, we had more freedom to practice with the persuasive mode. I wanted to give my students a prompt that would help them tap into issues that they felt were important—things they could get behind, feel strongly about, and persuade an audience to do. At the same time, I knew that persuasive writing could be tricky for adolescents. They are often full of passion and outrage but lack the maturity to objectively consider all sides of a topic. They often don't use logic and evidence, but instead just repeat their opinions, to defend their positions. However, because this group of students had demonstrated the ability to make thoughtful choices about writing and presentation, I decided to stretch their muscles.

First they would need to identify examples of persuasive writing all around them. I selected a few examples for them to explore on SimplyBox. As one student noted, "Oh, so persuasive writing is just telling what you think: not a fact, but an opinion." He tied this to his background knowledge of fact versus opinion.

Another student piped up, "But it has facts in it. The facts give more power to the author's opinion." The class nodded their heads in agreement.

In addition, I asked our school writing specialist, Staci Moore Hawkins, if she would focus on some persuasive and propaganda techniques during her one-hour weekly writing lab sessions. She was planning to begin a school newspaper, and these lessons worked right into her plans as well. After providing several real-world examples of persuasive writing and having students identify various techniques (such as using glittering generalities and the bandwagon effect, appealing to "plain folks" commonality, and fear), Staci asked small groups of students to create advertisements to perform for the class in order to give them some background knowledge of persuasive writing before we began our new project.

Although many of the persuasive techniques she taught wouldn't be appropriate for students' subsequent orations, they gave the students some firsthand experience reading, identifying, and performing persuasive writing.

Meanwhile, I searched for an example of persuasive writing that would also demonstrate the power of the spoken word and inspire them for our project focusing on important issues. Because YouTube had become such a great tutor for me in my technology education, I went there first. I found a video of a middle-grade student, Dalton Sherman, performing an award-winning oration ("Do You Believe in Me?") at the convocation for teachers in the Dallas public schools. He did an outstanding job of speaking and supporting his premise that students can do anything with the right inspiration and support.

Unfortunately, YouTube was blocked at school. Luckily, after searching for a few minutes, I discovered that the video clip was also on TeacherTube, which my students could view. (See Box 7.1 to learn more about gaining access to educational content on social networks and video sharing sites.)

An Instant Connection

My students instantly connected with the video of the "Do You Believe in Me?" speech. They were amazed that someone the same age could effectively communicate his message to a large audience of adults. Every word he selected and every inflection of his voice supported his message. They actually joined in clapping with the video audience at points he made in his oration. When the video concluded, half of my students were out of their seats, excited by his message.

This immediately segued into a class discussion, with students almost talking on top of one another because they were so inspired by what they had just seen.

Devante jumped up and exclaimed, "Mrs. Ramsay, I can do that! I did something like that at my church." (See an example of Devante's writing for this project in Figure 7.1.)

Rachel replied, "I can't believe he performed for such a big audience. He didn't seem nervous. He just felt what he was saying."

Box 7.1 | Removing Barriers to Learning

It's true that YouTube contains some inappropriate videos, but some are very educational. When I can't find a copy of a YouTube video on a school-approved site such as TeacherTube or SchoolTube, I often turn to a free file conversion tool called Zamzar. At www.zamzar.com, I copy the video's URL, select the type of file that I want to use for the download, type in my e-mail address, and click Convert. Zamzar will send the link to my e-mail address. Because the conversion process can be time-consuming and usually needs to take place on a home computer, I recommend not putting this off until you're trying to get out the door and off to school!

Another way to obtain videos for classroom use is by contacting the creators and asking them to post the videos on TeacherTube or other approved sites. When I explain how I will be using their work in my classroom, the creators usually are very gracious and sometimes send me the original files.

Don't be hesitant about asking for rights or permissions. The worst the creators can say is "no." Seeking permission in this way also models for students the importance of respecting the ownership of created materials and spurs rich discussions about digital citizenship (ISTE NETS for Students 5). Unfortunately, many teachers screen-capture images or videos without the owner's permission. They don't intend any harm, but they aren't honoring the work that went into the original creation and miss a golden opportunity to teach with their actions.

"I like the way that he kept repeating strongly the word *believe*," Elizabeth said. "Everyone knew that was his main meaning because of how he said it."

"He made you listen because of how his voice kept changing while he was speaking," Matthew agreed. "He must have spent a lot of time practicing his speech before performing."

Luna added, "He did an awesome job choosing the words when he wrote his speech."

From their comments, I could tell that they recognized that the boy wrote his material before he performed it and that his content and vocabulary choices had as much impact on his message as his body posture and voice inflection.

As we began discussing how they might do something similar, the conversation turned to audience. I asked, "For whom would you like to perform your writing?" I wanted them to make the decisions that would guide this project.

Some suggested their parents or other students in our school. But various work and class scheduling conflicts made those ideas difficult to enact. Then Rachel spoke up: "It would be really nice if we could share this with our e-pals." A chorus of "yes!" rose in reply.

I found it telling that my students immediately began thinking about their audience before they began planning the specifics of the project. It demonstrated an understanding that what and how we write depends on whom we're

FIGURE 7.1

Devante's Persuasive Writing

Underestimation

Have you ever been underestimated? Have I ever been underestimated? Do people underestimate us because of our age? The answer is yes. Even though kids like me are capable of so much, we are still underestimated.

Some people think that just because we are young, that we aren't capable of doing great things now. We are able to accomplish things like Skype, Jing, e-pals, podcast, and wikis in order to learn from people from all over the world. We know how to broaden our classroom's borders. We can go to the internet knowing where to go to find whatever we want to learn. You see I have more of a chance to go to college because of all the technology that we have access to now. If I wanted to learn another language, I could download it onto my mp3 player or I-pod and learn it now. I don't have to wait until high school or college. I can do this with any subject whatever, whenever, wherever. Knowing how to use all of these tools, taking control of our learning. We aren't treated like valuable citizens we are contributing citizens now . . . digital citizens.

I am here to say that you can never overestimate our potential. We are the future and the future begins now.

---

writing for. They realized that writing for adults would be different than writing for peers or younger students.

I already had a tool in mind for making their wish a reality. In one of the webinars that I had attended I learned about Skype, a tool that allows users to make free Internet calls, including video calls (see Box 7.2). I was excited that we had found a relevant way to incorporate this tool into a learning experience.

I contacted my teaching partner from the e-pals project and invited her to participate in what my students dubbed "The Oration Sensation." My students wanted to perform their writing for students in another state, seeing and hearing their audience in real time. Skype would give my students the opportunity to bring their communication full circle by blending their writing with their oral reading fluency as well as address language arts standards for oral persuasive presentations.

Box 7.2 | **Skype Conversations**

Skype allows registered users to make free calls through the Internet. Just sign up for an account, download the software, and you are ready to make calls. You will need a microphone so the other caller can hear you. If you want to make video calls, you will need to have a camera attached to your computer. Many computers already have these features built in. However, for best sound quality, I've found that an external microphone works best.

My students regularly make Skype calls now with our class Skype account. The computer is attached to our interactive whiteboard so that everyone in the room can see the callers. We set up the microphone to the computer and put the camera on a tripod (see Figure 7.2).

A day or two before we have scheduled a Skype conversation, the other teacher or speaker and I will plan a time to do a dry run to test our equipment and confirm the specifics of the conver-

sation. This usually eliminates most issues we might have so that anxious and excited students don't have a long wait just before the conversation.

My students not only share and perform their writing through Skype but also chat and ask questions of experts. Sometimes my students Skype with older students who can answer their question on a topic they are both studying at a different level of expertise. Other times they Skype with an author to discuss his or her writing. In addition, they use Skype to discuss their collaborative writing with peers across the country and to plan future writing endeavors.

Skype is an excellent tool for teachers to connect and plan collaboratively through the group call feature. I have also attended workshops conducted by Skype and have used Skype to converse with someone who can walk me through the steps of learning of a new technology tool.

FIGURE 7.2

Once More, This Time with Feeling

Now that they had chosen an audience, my students realized that they needed to write about topics that were close to their hearts so they could communicate a point of view with passion. They also agreed that they had to focus on issues they could realistically impact. One student suggested that although solving world hunger was a great idea, a ten-year-old can't make a difference in a few days, months, or even years. Instead she recommended setting small, achievable goals in an effort to get more students on board with their ideas.

In order to select their topics, each author conferenced with me and shared his or her ideas. I asked all of the students to justify why they felt strongly about their chosen issues. I guided them in selecting one that they felt strongest about before they returned to their seats to brainstorm and research facts to back up their claims. We followed the same process of having their peers read and respond to their writing throughout the writing process. In addition, they were to conference with me regularly, as time allowed, to come up with a polished final draft.

After writing the final versions of their stories, it was time to prepare for the oral part of their presentations. Although my students were quite fluent when recording a digital story, podcast, or VoiceThread, they were very hesitant initially to practice their orations. At first, I was confused. Then it hit me: They were so personally invested in the topics that they were afraid of judgment.

I decided to pull them into small groups to practice together with me. In this safe environment, they became more comfortable and felt free to give praise and suggestions for improvement. One day, during one of these small-group sessions, Elizabeth shared her speech about her cousin, Eli, a family favorite. Then she dropped a bomb: Eli had been shot by drug dealers. The point of her presentation was that you should be careful which friends you choose because they can really affect your future.

Before she could get much further in her speech, Joel stopped Elizabeth and asked, "Where was your cousin shot?" He had turned white as a sheet.

A surprised Elizabeth responded, "In the chest."

"No," Joel said, "I mean, where was he when he got shot?"

"In Mexico," Elizabeth answered.

Immediately Joel began sobbing. He explained that his three older brothers were drug dealers, and his initial fear when he heard Elizabeth speak was that one of his brothers had shot her cousin. Joel also shared that from a young age he had been instructed to spy on his brothers and report their activities back to his parents. He explained how difficult it had been because he felt responsible for their actions even though they were much older.

At this point Elizabeth and several other students were crying as well. The classroom became silent and something quite profound happened. The blanket of fear about sharing what they had written was lifted from the class. My students realized that they all had burdens. They started comforting one another, but they also realized the power their words had to heal or move someone to action.

No longer afraid of sharing their speeches, my students' oratory skills quickly improved. They often went back to the video that had initially inspired them, analyzing the speaker's techniques so they could apply the same strategies to their own performances. Often they asked to step out into the hallway to practice their presentations with one of their classmates.

Learning to Be Flexible

The scheduled time for the Oration Sensation on Skype was approaching. My students redecorated our classroom as a coffee shop. They brought in table-cloths and refreshments, including mugs full of lemon-lime soda; no coffee, because they said it would make them all hyper and they were excited enough.

Then, two days before the event, I got an e-mail message from my partner teacher saying that her school would not let her use Skype because of safety concerns. I could only imagine the looks on my students' faces when they learned this. I had to find a solution fast.

I signed onto Second Life (see Chapter 2). As luck would have it, my Maine pal Mary O'Brien was online. I sent her a message and posed my problem. She said that she had never used Skype before, but she was willing to try it. We discussed some of the logistics and she set about making preparations on her end. After a couple of e-mail messages back and forth, we decided to do a test run the following day.

I shared the change of plans with my students. At first, they were confused and upset because they had kept a certain group of students in mind when they were writing and practicing their orations. But when I told them about their new audience and how eager they were to participate, they relaxed and started planning anew. While eating lunch, they barely talked because they were mentally concentrating on the upcoming experience. When we returned to our "coffee house," you could feel the energy in the air.

Watching my students passionately share their writing went beyond my imagination. (In Box 7.3, Mary O'Brien describes the effect of the presentations on her third graders.) Priscilla had been emotionally moved when she saw a story about a girl her age who had been riding her bike in her neighborhood and had disappeared. She felt strongly that everyone needed to take precautions

---

| Box 7.3 | **The Perspective from Maine** |

I had the pleasure of meeting Julie Ramsay at the International Society for Technology in Education in the virtual world of Second Life. We connected immediately, and I soon recognized her as a talented and dedicated educator. Shortly after our meeting, Julie invited my third-grade class to Skype with her fifth graders in order to give them an audience for their persuasive writing. I agreed because it sounded interesting, and technology is my thing. The result was truly inspirational.

Her students had written poetry, speeches, and stories that had a lesson. Julie wisely suggested that we add a segment to personalize the Skype meeting, with each student sharing a fact about their respective states. We developed the format of, "Did you know (insert interesting fact) about Maine/Alabama?" Her students were sweet and sensitive to my younger students. After this brief introduction, her students shared their writing. I was deeply moved by their writing and the messages they shared. It was evident that Julie

had given these young people a true reason for writing and the self-confidence necessary to communicate such deep and important ideas.

My students were amazed by what they heard and saw. Because they were younger and from a small town in Maine, they couldn't believe the topics generated by the more mature kids from Alabama. For some of my students, who are geographically isolated, this was also their first experience hearing a Southern accent.

Because of our collaboration on Skype, my students were inspired to write something themselves, a piece that might make a difference in the world. They realized that writing can carry an important message that is relevant to someone in Alabama, Maine, or almost anywhere. Using Skype enabled my students to get a better sense of the bigger world.

—Mary O'Brien
Manchester Elementary School
Manchester, Maine

---

to keep themselves safe, even close to home. T'Kiya spoke about animal cruelty. She has a beloved dog named Penny that she couldn't imagine her life without. She had seen and heard so much about people being cruel to stray animals and she wanted everyone to protect these animals. Rachel has such a compassionate heart that when she overheard someone talking negatively about a special needs student, she really wanted people to realize that everyone deserves respect regardless of ability level. Sam wanted people to be valued because of their inside qualities, not on their outside appearance.

My students showed they knew how to analyze a problem (personal to global) and break it down to find a solution that they could implement now. They skillfully wrote and created using different genres—poetry, speeches, and short stories with a moral—for an audience of peers. They each chose a topic that fit them as authors, not a common theme that was dictated by me. All of this happened because of writing that they designed, composed, and performed. Oh yes, and technology was part of the process too.

CHAPTER

8

Learning Far and Near

Standards and Skills
- Communication and collaboration
- Creativity
- Oral reading fluency: articulation
- Technology operations and concepts
- Critical thinking and problem solving

Technology Tools
- Digital video camera
- Windows Movie Maker (software)

As each school year draws to a close, I find myself feeling reflective. I wonder about the lessons that I did not have time for in the schedule. I evaluate the projects that went well and those that didn't, vowing to improve and make changes the next year. Above all, I reflect on the progress of my students. How will they fare in the future? Have I given them everything that they need to succeed once they leave our classroom?

With the school year described in this book having been much different in focus than previous ones, I wondered how these students in particular would manage in the following grades. Would they have the knowledge, experience, and confidence to boldly tackle whatever academic or personal challenges they might face?

Like many educators, I fight the inner struggle of wanting to hold on to my students a bit longer to teach one more lesson, give another dose of encouragement, light one more spark. But I also want to let them leave and be free to soar to new heights as independent learners.

The Final Countdown

As we reached the final week of school, my students happily clambered in each morning, many of them continuing to arrive before the official start time even though all of our assignments had been completed and grades posted. Other classes may have viewed movies or completed worksheets in the final days of the semester. My enthusiastic learners got out past learning games and activities and busily worked together, often insisting that I leave my monstrously long end-of-school list and join them.

One morning I noticed several of my students sitting at a table, heads together, deep in a discussion. Everyone seemed quietly engaged in this conversation so I didn't interrupt. Within a few minutes, however, they approached me with an idea. They had seen some videos on YouTube (at home) of students talking about digital citizenship. They had been discussing what they liked about the productions and concluded that they needed to create a digital video to summarize what our class had accomplished during the school year.

I loved this idea, but I knew that they had no experience with digital video and only had five days left to finish whatever they started. Yet I could only laugh and marvel at them once more; their enthusiasm and confidence were so infectious. They never doubted their ability to complete this task with the tools at hand in such a tight time frame.

This reinforced much of what we had been doing throughout the year, when they designed and created projects where they could investigate and make deeper connections to a topic. We had been moving toward more of a project-based learning approach in our classroom (see Box 8.1), and this was how my students wanted to spend their final days together.

Here's Our Plan

Of course, from their experience, my students knew they would need a specific plan. They started to explain their ideas—many voices expressing one intention.

"We know that this has to have content," Sean started. "It can't be just for fun."

Elizabeth chimed in, "We know that we have to teach something with our writing."

Box 8.1 Project-Based Learning

Project-based learning is a method of instructing across content areas, using inquiry to tap into students' multiple interests and intelligences. Well-designed projects keep students at the center of the decision-making process in determining the specifics of their projects and usually their assessment. The teacher's role is to be a facilitator, not the director. Within the context of the project, students make connections and reach a deeper understanding of content standards through a variety of activities along the project's path to completion. Learners typically apply their learning to a real-world problem or situation. I had been guiding my students in this direction for several years because I found that with project-based learning I was able to reach those with different ability levels and learning preferences better than with traditional instruction. Typically, these projects require more than a couple of class periods to complete and require collaboration among team members, who must dig into facts or data before producing their findings.

Here are some jumping-off points for investigating project-based learning:

- Common Craft Project-Based Learning (www.commoncraft.com/project-based-learning-explained-custom_video-project-bie)
- Edutopia (www.edutopia.org/project-based-learning)
- PBL Exemplary Projects (www.wested.org/pblnet/exemplary_projects.html)
- Problem and Project Based Learning Activities (www.mrsoshouse.com/pbl/pblin.html)
- Houghton Mifflin's Project-Based Learning Space (http://college.cengage.com/education/pbl/project/project.html)
- An Innovation Odyssey Story Finder (http://educate.intel.com/odyssey/StoryFinder.aspx?viewby=category)

You'll note that some projects require deeper thinking and problem solving than others. I have tinkered with some projects that I found at the sites listed above, but in general my students prefer to design and implement their own ideas. You might explore the published descriptions at these sites to get some ideas and then set off on your own student-directed learning adventures.

Sean continued, "We'd like to write a poem to express what we've done this year, especially with our e-pals."

Rachel added, "We could write a poem based on Henry Wadsworth Longfellow's 'The Midnight Ride of Paul Revere'" (see Chapter 3).

Ashlyn continued, "Since Sean is really talented at writing poetry, we thought he could write the rough draft with the ideas we all brainstorm. Then we can work together to edit, adding all of our thoughts and ideas."

"We know that we have to have the poem written and edited before we even think about publishing it as a digital video," Rachel added. "Is it okay if we do this, Mrs. Ramsay?"

Do you ever have moments in your classroom when you wonder if something really happened or if you dreamed it? This was one of those moments for me. My authors demonstrated an understanding of the importance and place for writing, collaborating, and creating with technology tools in order to express themselves. In my mind, we had come to the end of a very successful year. In their minds, they felt the need to wrap up and express their thoughts and feelings about our experiences as a classroom community.

I was overjoyed not only because they understood the relevance of writing and creating in their lives but also because they recognized the power of technology to give voice to their ideas. They needed to express themselves and articulate their gratitude to their friends on the other side of the country, who had become their partners in their learning journey this year.

First Things First

I was still concerned about how we were going to find the time to complete this project, but I wholeheartedly encouraged the students to begin work and stepped back, letting them take complete control. After brainstorming some of the highlights of the year, they immediately pulled out a copy of the original text of "The Midnight Ride of Paul Revere" to begin planning.

The students gave Sean a couple of hours to write; they checked on his progress, occasionally making suggestions and always offering words of encouragement. When Sean finished the first draft, three other students sat with him, adding new ideas and editing the poem so it had the feel of the original text. When they had a version they were comfortable with, they brought it to me to review and offer suggestions.

The maturity of writing in that composition took me by surprise. I knew they had become accomplished authors across content areas, modes, and genres. We had been writing constantly throughout the year and I had charted their progress. I knew how much they had grown, more so than any other class that I had taught. But what surfaced with this presentation went beyond the eloquence of talented fifth graders. They had managed to summarize the year's accomplishments while staying true to the original inspiration of Longfellow's poem:

Learning Far and Near

Listen my children and you shall hear,
Of the learning time from far and near,
On the twenty-ninth of May in '09,
Every digital citizen is still alive,
Who remembers the famous project we did,
We said to the world "Joy, Joy we,
Have done everything alive. Like digital stories,

Wikis, Jing, READ posters, scanner collages,
Tech and writing projects, more, more, and more."
Our communications both back and forth
Traveled across from our Alabama school
Digitally riding to the Peoria Bay
Right when the sun,
Rose over the day where to our writing,
And ideas you never said "Nay."
The writer's block never came,
As we wrote to you for ever more,
A worldly collaboration with each letter,
Across the sky like a rainbow,
And a huge experience that was magnified
By flattening of classroom walls in our stride,
While everyone went through the valley of learning from another,
And we stayed on track and never,
Missed an opportunity to teach or learn.
Others wonder how we do it
But it takes lots of effort with us two,
We worked together in a quest for the best.
That's why we say unto you thanks,
For a year that will stand out as the best!

—Sean (inspired by Henry Wadsworth Longfellow's
"The Midnight Ride of Paul Revere")

(*Note:* To view the full digital video production, see www.stenhouse.com/
skiplunch.)

Other educators have seen this example of collaborative writing and usually
make the assumption that I directed the entire writing process, that I was very
hands-on. The opposite is true. Except for a few minor changes, the entire
poem was composed and directed by ten- and eleven-year-old students drawing
on their previous creating and collaborating experiences.

Final Production

Now it was time to publish their work. Before they ever asked about technology tools and how to create a digital video, they pulled everyone together
and planned who would perform each part of the poem. Then they began
practicing with one another to gain oral fluency and expression and to learn
their lines. They decided that everyone must memorize their lines so that the

audience would not be distracted by them holding a note card or piece of paper. Was I in the room? Absolutely, but this time I was almost entirely an observer.

After all that planning and practicing, they approached me and asked for the equipment. I pulled out the digital video recorder I had purchased with a classroom stipend. I taught them how to use the camera and showed them how to attach it to the tripod that I had also purchased.

While several of the students were learning how to use the camera, others were making plans for the background. The set designers wanted the video to be simple, not flashy, because their words were most important. They knew that I still had the blue tablecloths that they used for our Oration Sensation coffeehouse, so they asked if they could use them. They went into a corner of the classroom, moved desks, and stretched one of the tablecloths from the top of the bulletin board to our hanging television so it would be taller than all of them.

Toward the end of the day, they met together and decided that they all needed to wear white shirts so they would show up well on the camera in front of the dark background. They gave each other assignments to practice their parts of the poem.

When I arrived at school the next morning, I had my usual welcoming committee waiting for me at my classroom door. They showed me the final draft and presented their plans for the day. They set up the equipment and set and decided who would perform the different production roles. Ashyln took charge to ensure they had camera operators, directors, and assistants to work with people on their scripts before they went in front of the camera. She also organized the participants in the correct order. The directors made simple cue cards in case someone got stage fright in front of the camera.

They encouraged one another when they made mistakes, applauded when someone finished a clip, and watched patiently, giving advice as needed. It took the students only forty-five minutes to finish the filming. Initially, I expected it to take them the better part of a day. I was expecting that my role, besides being an occasional advisor, would be to help them manage their time on this project. However, the time-management skills that they had learned from our previous collaborations really carried the day. What an important life skill for them to have learned how to master!

From Many to One

After connecting the video camera to the laptop and downloading the various video clips, Elizabeth wanted to learn video editing. We used Windows Movie Maker, simple video editing software that was already installed on our laptop, to link the clips together.

By "we," I mean that I showed her the few basics that I knew how to use and she built upon that knowledge to learn and experiment with the different features. (Box 8.2 provides information on learning about video editing.) She sat at the back table and became totally engrossed in finding the best takes, chopping unneeded space, and trying to blend the takes into one seamless video. Her peers would periodically sit beside her, watching and asking questions about the different features or why she made certain choices. Without missing a beat, Elizabeth answered their questions or demonstrated how something worked and then continued. When she hit a roadblock, she figured out a solution. When the announcement was made that it was time for dismissal, Elizabeth wasn't ready to go home; she wanted to keep going until she had finished. I reassured her that everything would be waiting for her when she arrived at school the next morning.

The following morning, after Elizabeth finished editing the clips together, Rachel and Sean added the title and ending credits and imported music. They insisted that the other students preview the video and make any last suggestions. Finally, using the Windows Movie Maker software, they converted the video to a Windows Media Player file so we could upload it to our class Web site for their e-pals to view.

Box 8.2 Digital Video Production with Students

If you are like me, you may shy away from video production with students because it seems so time-consuming. This is definitely not a project (if done correctly, with the proper focus on content creation) that students can complete in a few class periods or even a week. Because our project was done at the end of the year, they had the freedom to work throughout the day.

We used Windows Movie Maker because that was what we had available. My friends who use Apple computers have told me that iMovie is easy to use as well. My students were standing close to the camera, so the built-in microphone on our camera worked for our purpose. We did not use voice-overs. If you want to experiment with voice-overs, Audacity (see Chapter 6) records, mixes, and edits sounds that can be imported into the software. Windows Movie Maker makes it easy to add text titles and credits as well as import copyright-free music from sites such as Freeplay Music (http://freeplaymusic.com).

If you feel overwhelmed (as I did) and don't know where to begin, a few helpful resources can guide your students. The focus of most of the following Web sites is the production side of projects. My students demonstrated that the content and message were most important; the tools just brought their voices to life.

- Kids' Vid (http://kidsvid.4teachers.org/index.shtml)
- Multimedia Seeds (http://eduscapes.com/seeds/production/editdigital.html)
- Digital Video in Education (http://edtech.guhsd.net/video.html)

The Answer to My Question

That final day of production, the students watched their video many, many times. They jokingly bemoaned that they did not have any popcorn for their viewing pleasure. Each student enjoyed taking credit for his or her part and praising peers for their contributions.

I remembered the nagging questions that I had in my head three days before: Would they have the knowledge, experience, and confidence to boldly tackle whatever academic or personal challenges they might face? The answer was a resounding "Yes!" They demonstrated knowledge of writing (while meeting state standards) for an authentic purpose and audience. They found a tool that would bring their words to life. They worked collaboratively and used their creativity to communicate to their friends across the country. My learners used their knowledge of technology concepts and operations and applied them to new situations using their critical-thinking and problem-solving skills to create a digital video that fulfilled their need to summarize their experiences that school year. They did all of this while being kind, professional, and conscious of the time, exhibiting a strong, self-driven work ethic (ISTE NETS for Students 1, 2, 4, and 6).

What will the future be like with students like these leading and making decisions? They are already fashioning the present at ages ten and eleven. It's hard to imagine the possibilities.

While my learners expressed an unwillingness to leave our classroom learning community because of all we had accomplished, I knew that I was the one who had received the best gift. I learned so much more from them by letting go of control and placing it in their capable hands. They had empowered me as an educator to freely try new things and trust my instincts about how to guide them by paying attention to their interests and addressing their individual learning needs. We met state and national standards, but we also set new standards as learners on a global frontier.

What is exciting is that each school year is a different journey with unique challenges and opportunities. The constant is our students; they are at the center of all learning and should be part of every plan to bring them to a higher level of knowledge. Will you join me in listening to their voices and releasing their enthusiasm and talents to the world? Imagine the possibilities.

References

Alabama State Department of Education. 2007. *Alabama Course of Study: English Language Arts.* Montgomery, AL: Alabama State Department of Education.

Applebee, A. N., and J. A. Langer. 2006. *The State of Writing Instruction in America's Schools: What Existing Data Tell Us.* Albany, NY: Center on English Learning and Achievement, University at SUNY, Albany. http://www.albany.edu/cela/reports.html.

Barrett, Helen C. 2009. "How to Create Simple Digital Stories." http://electronicportfolios.com/digistory/howto.html.

Clements, Andrew. 1998. *Frindle.* New York: Aladdin.

Curtis, Christopher Paul. 2002. *Bud, Not Buddy.* New York: Yearling.

Federal Trade Commission. 2010. *Net Cetera: Chatting with Kids About Being Online.* OnGuard Online. http://www.onguardonline.gov/pdf/tec04.pdf.

ISTE (International Society for Technology in Education). 2007. "Standards: NETS for Students 2007." ISTE. http://www.iste.org/standards/nets-for-students/nets-student-standards-2007.aspx.

L'Engle, Madeleine. 1962. *A Wrinkle in Time.* New York: Macmillan.

Longfellow, Henry Wadsworth. 2008. "The Midnight Ride of Paul Revere." In *Reading Street: Grade 5.* Glenview, IL: Pearson Education.

Metiri Group. 2008. *Multimodal Learning Through Media: What the Research Says.* San Jose, CA: Cisco. http://www.cisco.com/web/strategy/docs/education/Multimodal-Learning-Through-Media.pdf.

NCTE/IRA (National Council of Teachers of English and International Reading Association). 1996. *The Standards for the English Language Arts.* Urbana, IL: NCTE and Newark, DE: IRA.

O'Dell, Scott. 1987. *Island of the Blue Dolphins.* New York: Yearling.

Partnership for 21st Century Skills. 2004. *A Framework for 21st Century Learning.* Tucson, AZ: Partnership for 21st Century Skills.

Porter, Bernajean. 2010. "Where's the Beef? Adding Rigor to Student Digital Products." *Learning & Leading with Technology* 38 (2): 14–17.

University of Houston. 2010. "The Educational Uses of Digital Storytelling." University of Houston. http://digitalstorytelling.coe.uh.edu/.

Wormeli, Rick. 2006. *Fair Isn't Always Equal: Assessing and Grading in the Differentiated Classroom.* Portland, ME: Stenhouse.

———. 2007. *Differentiation: From Planning to Practice, Grades 6–12.* Portland, ME: Stenhouse.

Index